LET IT
BLEED

LET IT BLEED

The Rolling Stones, Altamont, and the End of the Sixties

ETHAN A. RUSSELL

WITH GERARD VAN DER LEUN

SPRINGBOARD PRESS

NEW YORK   BOSTON

SPRINGBOARD PRESS
Hachette Book Group
237 Park Avenue, New York, NY 10017

Visit our Web site at www.HachetteBookGroup.com

Printed in China

First Edition: November 2009
10 9 8 7 6 5 4 3 2 1

Springboard Press is an imprint of Grand Central Publishing.
The Springboard Press name and logo are trademarks of Hachette Book Group, Inc.

Library of Congress Cataloging-in-Publication Data

Russell, Ethan A.
  Let It Bleed : the Rolling Stones, Altamont, and the end of the sixties / Ethan A. Russell, with Gerard Van der Leun.—1st ed.
    p. cm.
  ISBN: 978-0-446-53904-3
  1. Rolling Stones. 2. Rock musicians—England—Biography. 3. Altamont Festival (1969 : Livermore, Calif.) I. Van der Leun, Gerard, 1945– II. Title.
  ML421.R64R87 2006
  782.42166092'2—dc22
  [B]   2008053229

Design: Roger Gorman, Reiner Design Consultants

This book is dedicated to my generation,
To my fellow travelers from the tour,
And with love to my family,
Shannon, Gabriel, and Lucas.

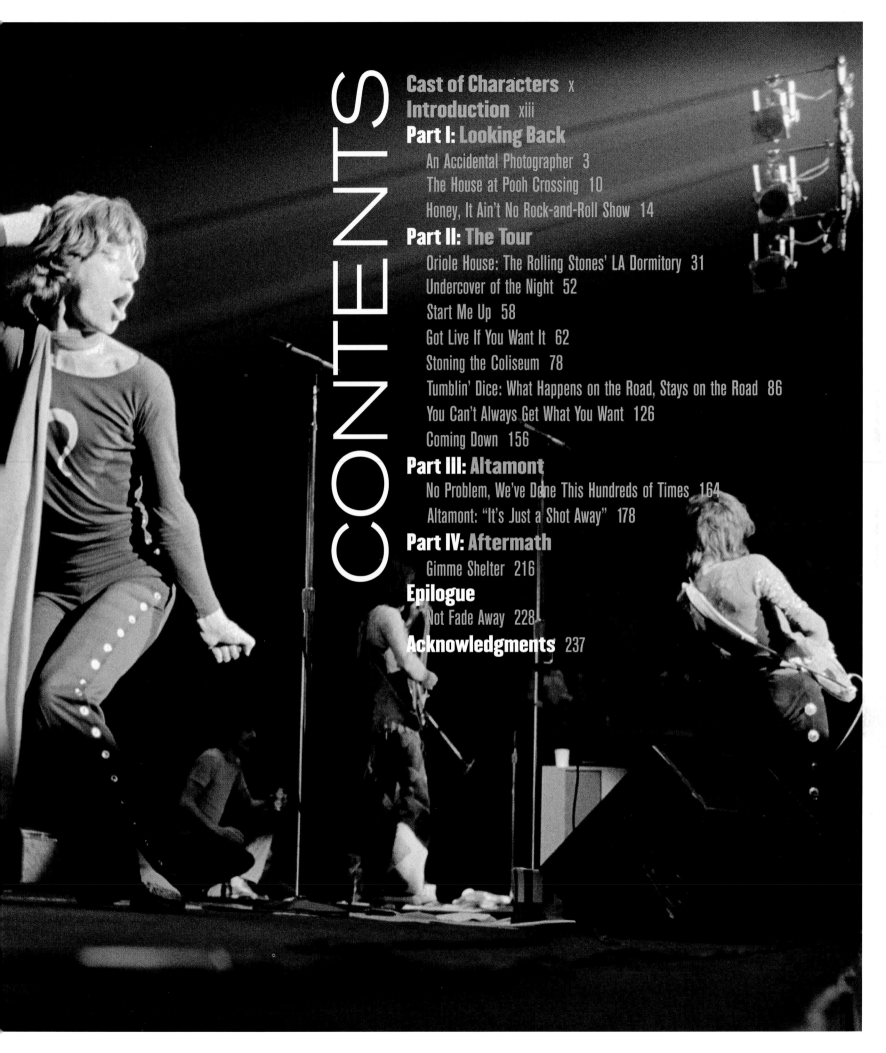

CONTENTS

TOUR DATES

November 7, 1969
Colorado State University, Fort Collins, CO

November 8, 1969
Inglewood Forum, Los Angeles, CA

November 9, 1969
Alameda County Coliseum, Oakland, CA

November 10, 1969
Sports Arena, San Diego, CA

November 11, 1969
Coliseum, Phoenix, AZ

November 13, 1969
Moody Coliseum, Dallas, TX

November 14, 1969
University of Alabama Coliseum, Auburn, AL

November 15, 1969
Assembly Hall, University of Illinois, Champaign, IL

November 16, 1969
International Amphitheatre, Chicago, IL

November 24, 1969
Olympia Stadium, Detroit, MI

November 25, 1969
Spectrum Sports Arena, Philadelphia, PA

November 26, 1969
Baltimore Civic Center, Baltimore, MD

November 27, 1969
Madison Square Garden, New York, NY

November 28, 1969
Madison Square Garden, New York, NY

November 29, 1969
Boston Garden, Boston, MA

November 30, 1969
International Raceway, West Palm Beach, FL

December 6, 1969
Altamont Speedway, Livermore, CA

Cast of Characters

Mick Jagger Singer/Performer (English)

The son of a physical education instructor, Mick Jagger was born on July 26, 1943, in Dartford, Kent, England. The 1969 US tour was his—and the Stones'—first in three years. A Rolling Stone since 1962, Jagger and the Stones played Rio de Janeiro in 2006 before a million and a half people.

Keith Richards Guitarist (English)

Keith Richards, an only child, was born in Dartford, Kent, December 18, 1943. Keith—with Mick Jagger—joined Ian Stewart and Brian Jones to form the Rolling Stones. Ronnie Schneider: "I could give you a million stories about Keith being a man's man. I remember a guy comes up and bothers Charlie's wife and Keith smashes him over the head with a beer bottle, while holding a baby, as he pushes the guy down the stairs."

Bill Wyman Bass Guitarist (English)

Born in 1936, Bill Wyman joined the original Rolling Stones in 1962. He played with them until 1993. He is famous for his expressionless immobility onstage. ("I've never met anyone who moved less than Bill, but he added to the act tremendously," says Chip Monck. Bill demurs, "I used to sweat a little bit under me arms.") Since his departure in 1993, Bill has published several books and still performs and records. He has three young daughters and a fully grown son, Stephen.

Charlie Watts Drummer (English)

The thing about Charlie Watts, a remarkable legacy, is how everyone feels motivated to offer such kind observations about him: "The only one, a staunch friend over the years." "There's such a serene, calm goodness about Charlie." "Charlie was very down-to-earth." He was not playing "I am a great Rolling Stone, rock star." I once heard somebody say, "You're on the road the whole time. God, it must be hard." Charlie replied, "Jesus, musicians have been doing this since the dawn of time. We've got it easy." Charlie Watts was born in Islington on June 2, 1941.

Mick Taylor Guitarist (English)

Born January 17, 1949, in Welwyn Garden City, Hertfordshire, England. In 1969 Mick Taylor was recruited to replace Brian Jones, and his addition allowed the Stones to tour again. Bill Wyman: "Mick Taylor became the most musical person in the band, more technically clever than all the rest of us. We were just musicians, basically, and he was way above us in his technique. But he fitted very well." Mick Taylor left the Stones in 1974. He lives in England, still performs and records.

Ian Stewart Pianist (Scots)

Brian Jones placed the ad, and Ian Stewart answered it. That was the beginning of the Rolling Stones. Born in Pittenweem in the East Neuk, Scotland, in 1938, Stu was asked to leave the band by their then manager, Andrew Loog Oldham. He did not look the part, though that was not the reason given. But Stu stayed with them for the rest of his life. He died in England in 1985. On the 1969 tour Stu did what he always did: helped get the band on the stage, performed with them, and was, as Stanley Booth puts it, "the only grown-up." When I saw Stu on stage at Altamont, it was the first time I had ever seen him worried. I knew then we were in trouble.

Ronnie Schneider Tour Manager (American)

Born in New Jersey in 1943, Ronnie Schneider grew up in Miami. ("With that 'let's party' mentality. You have good weather. You go to the beach. You get a suntan. You pick up girls. I loved it.") He was on the road with the Stones in 1966. In 1969 Mick Jagger called and asked him to do the tour without involving Ronnie's uncle, Allen Klein.

Sam Cutler Personal Tour Manager (English)

Born in London's East End, Sam lost his parents in the Second World War. He was placed in an orphanage but was later adopted. "At fifteen I left home, school, and England, having already suffered three mothers and four fathers." As much as any individual, Sam took the fall for Altamont, about which he's still angry. Ronnie Schneider: "Sam had to disappear—he went into hiding for quite a long time. He was the most hardworking guy that I've ever met. He was definitely driven—I think he was absolutely fantastic at what he did." The interviews with Sam began in 2000 and were completed in 2006. He's a central figure, with interesting facets to his story. Sam is married with two children and lives in Australia.

Georgia "Jo" Bergman
Assistant/Office Manager (American)

Born in Oakland in 1945, Jo Bergman ran the Rolling Stones office in London and went on the road with them on multiple tours from 1968 through 1972. During those years little that had anything to do with the Rolling Stones was outside her purview. She left to go to Warner Bros. Records, becoming its only female vice president by the time she retired. She lives in Altadena, California.

Astrid Lundstrom (Swedish)

Born in a small village in northern Sweden in 1947, Astrid traveled by boat to England in 1966. Within her first month there she was to meet George Harrison, Paul McCartney, Jimi Hendrix, and Bill Wyman. She and Bill were together for seventeen years, and she accompanied him on every tour. "Other than them [the Rolling Stones] I was the only one who was there the whole time." Today Astrid lives in Tucson, Arizona.

Stanley Booth Writer (American)

In 1969 Stanley Booth received from the Rolling Stones "their exclusive cooperation in putting together a book about the Rolling Stones." He devoted fifteen years of his life to writing it. *The True Adventures of the Rolling Stones* has been called by Peter Guralnick "the one authentic masterpiece of rock 'n' roll writing." About it Keith Richards says, "Stanley's book is the only one I can read and say, yeah, that's how it was." Born in Georgia in 1942, Stanley first met the Rolling Stones in 1968. Still writing, Stanley lives in Brunswick, Georgia, with his wife, Diann.

Ethan Russell Photographer (American)

Born in New York in 1945, Ethan grew up in San Francisco. He went to London in 1967 as part of a European summer vacation. He stayed, working initially as a volunteer with autistic children while trying to be a writer. He had taken a few photos in college. Seen by a young journalist writing for a new magazine called *Rolling Stone*, he was asked if he wanted to photograph Mick Jagger. He photographed the Rolling Stones during the years 1968–1972. He also photographed the Beatles, the Who, and many others. Today he lives in Marin County with his wife, stepson, and five-year-old son.

Michael Lydon Writer (American)

Michael Lydon was the second writer on the tour. Michael's physical appearance and lifestyle (over-the-shoulder hair, jeans, living in Mendocino) all said "hippie." His demeanor was so unassuming that it totally obscured the fact, which I found out during our interview, that he was a reporter for the *New York Times*, for *Newsweek*, for *Esquire*—and was a graduate of Yale. Michael was delightful then and is now. He is a working musician and music teacher in New York City.

Chip Monck Stage and Lighting Designer (American)

Chip Monck had a certain degree of personal notoriety before he joined the 1969 tour; among other things, he was the "voice of Woodstock" due to his multiple appearances in the movie *Woodstock* speaking to the crowd, warning them, among other things, of "bad acid." His interview reveals that lighting and staging were, more or less, everything to him before and after the Stones 1969 Tour. He now lives in Australia.

Tony Funches "Security" (American)

A Vietnam vet and the son of two religious parents, Tony was the president of the West Los Angeles College when someone asked him if he wanted to help look out for the Rolling Stones while they were in LA. "My job was to sit in my Volkswagen down by the gate." It didn't last. Once they got to know Tony, the Stones asked him to come on the tour. At Altamont he broke two bones in his hand knocking out Hells Angels. "That I lived is still a surprise to me." I interviewed Tony in Hendersonville, Nevada, in 2006.

Jon Jaymes "Transportation" (American)

Jon Jaymes, aka John Ellsworth, materialized at the beginning of the tour claiming to be from the Chrysler Corporation. To Chrysler he said he was working with the Stones. Newspaper accounts described him as a promoter of allegedly bogus businesses from eucalyptus plantations to European hamburger joints. His exploits were extraordinary, including appearing at the Carter White House as Santa Claus while attempting to defraud a children's charity.

Introduction

There were only sixteen of us, including the five Rolling Stones, and our average age was twenty-six. We were from Sweden, London's East End, Boston, the Okefenokee Swamp, East LA, San Francisco, Miami. We were English, American, Scots, Swedish, and middle-class, privileged, poor, black, idealistic, and criminal. We flew—can you imagine today?—commercial airlines.

The Rolling Stones 1969 US Tour was a remarkable tour at a remarkable time. ("The last music tour," I call it.) The 1960s were a unique era, the likes of which we shall not see again. Some say Altamont—the free concert tacked on to the end of the tour—ended the sixties. Not everyone shares that perception nor has the same sense of how we did as a generation, but that story is still being lived.

Since I was the photographer for the tour I had an inside view of the sometimes-almost-ecstatic experience of the sixteen scheduled shows and the nightmare that was Altamont. "It was the best of times. It was the worst of times" is a tempting quote.

I am an American, a person who was swept up by the music and came to believe in what it meant to my generation. Altamont brought most of that crashing to the ground. Many Americans of that era express this sentiment, but most often the English do not. It is interesting, this divide along national lines (and predictable, if we knew then what we know now). To speak perhaps too broadly, the Americans were crushed and the English didn't get it. The net result was we faded away.

Like every generation, you move on. What are your choices? But I was never comfortable with this feeling of collapse. I was not alone. The Eagles, in the tradition of that era, would write, "You call someplace paradise / Kiss it good-bye."

Let It Bleed began as a fairly straightforward re-creation of a remarkable tour. As I assembled the book, it grew to be more. Reviewing the photographs, and reading and talking about it with my colleagues, I soon came to understand that the project couldn't avoid the unanswered question: "What went wrong?" That question lingered because it was never examined but instead had been met with either minimization, denial, or blame.

If you think you know the story, you don't. Many of the people speaking here are talking for the first time, and they are speaking across a broad span of years with a perspective that would have never been possible immediately, or even a decade, after the fact.

As I was conducting the interviews for this book I discovered how little I really knew about the people who shared this extraordinary experience with me, some of whom had been my friends for forty years. I also learned how that one fateful day, December 6, 1969, affected us all. People had their memories from the tour, although they were diffuse, as seen through the fog of time. But when the conversation turned to Altamont, everyone remembered it as if it were yesterday.

Bill Wyman was the oldest, born in London's East End in 1936, and Mick Taylor the youngest, born just north of London in 1949. As a young boy, Stanley Booth (born in 1942 near the Okefenokee Swamp, in Georgia) lay in bed listening to the sound of the wind in the Turpentine Woods. And Astrid Lundstrom spent her summers on an idyllic family farm in the north of Sweden. You could easily imagine that lives as disparate as ours, as geographically separate, would never cross. What could bring us together, what could we possibly have in common? As was so often the case in the sixties, it was— at the beginning and in the end—the music.

Bill Wyman was in the Royal Air Force, stationed in Germany, when he first heard rock 'n' roll on American Armed Forces Radio, but it was seeing Chuck Berry in the movie *Rock, Rock, Rock* that sealed his fate. "The hair stood up on the back of my head, and I got shivers all over. I'd never been affected like that. I think Keith [Richards] saw that movie about sixteen times!" And Mick Jagger was carrying *Rockin' at the Hops*, a Chuck Berry record, under his arm when he and Keith bumped into each other at the Dartford train station and decided to get together.

Stanley Booth was driving with his parents across Georgia when he first heard Ella Mae Morse on the radio. "It was out of the night in South Georgia. It was just as black as the inside of your hat. And I thought, 'Damn, I don't know what this is. But this is what I want!' "

In San Francisco I lay in bed listening to the foghorns out the window and to the soft country music on my brown plastic monaural radio—the orange glow of the tubes shining through the cracks in the back. Then Elvis appeared and swept me into rock 'n' roll, which introduced me to Little Richard, Chuck Berry, and the Everly Brothers.

I sometimes think of the sixteen of us as passengers boarding separate trains at stations continents apart, but over time the train lines converged until we were deposited on top of a hill in Los Angeles in 1969. Then all of us, on the same train, embarked across America, until on December 6, 1969, we arrived, with 300,000 others, at a location no one had ever heard of, a series of brown hills forty miles east of San Francisco.

As Michael Lydon, a writer from the tour, remembers, it was a time when "the number of ideas were moving around very rapidly, and very brilliantly. It was an emerging international conversation about life, and art, and music, and politics. It wasn't directed, but inspired by brilliant statements of all kinds—trenchant, challenging observations. Jerry Garcia was as smart as one of your friends from Yale who was a clerk for some Supreme Court judge. No, even smarter. The more I listened to the music and the ideas they generated, and the more I got into it, I just felt a personal challenge from it. Bob Dylan sang: 'He not busy being born is busy dying . . .' I took that as a challenge. If you're not really fighting to keep growing, you're going to wither away. So if I don't want to wither away, I've got to keep growing. I wanted to be part of the conversation. I wanted to write about it. I wanted to make my own contribution."

In the sweltering South, Stanley Booth spent an afternoon with the Beatles in the summer of 1966: "It was one thing to hear their records and enjoy that, but then you meet them, and they're four different people—not just some pop phenomenon. Four guys who do what they do rather well, and they're just like us. You realized that something was going on, an international phenomenon, and it was going someplace. It appeared that there was a very positive energy that people were participating in; that was passing between these characters, whether it was Antonioni or Truffaut, the Stones or Dylan, Joan Baez. There was this attitude, and it was a positive attitude; it was a prohuman attitude and an attitude of genuine values. I mean when John Lennon asked the mayor of Liverpool, 'When are you going to get those people some teeth?' That was just great. It was sensible and it gave one hope."

IN LONDON, GEORGIA "JO" BERGMAN LENT PAUL MCCARTNEY her makeup and wondered why he needed it for a radio show. Before that she had worked in the theater and witnessed the explosion of fashion and ideas, and the emergence of Britain from the Second World War: "It was really exciting, just the best time. Nineteen sixty-two was the beginning. In '63 it really started exploding. Not just the Beatles—that's when the fashion started happening and the films and the art and everything else. In England what had happened in the sixties is an upending of some of the expectations of the class system. Talented people—from Liverpool, or the East End, or from anywhere that was working-class or lower-middle-class—became photographers, filmmakers, fashion designers, actors, or musicians. They came bursting through the door, just threw it open. Suddenly, popular culture, which had been ersatz American, was upended by all of these people saying 'Wait a minute' and doing it with humor and wit and style, and all of it came together, and that's what was so exciting about being in England in the sixties: just this profusion of surprise in every creative media that you looked at—in every form that you looked at. It was just enormously exciting to be there. And we all knew it. It was the beginning of practically everything."

"The music came across the airwaves," says Keith Richards, "and suddenly it felt like the world was actually changing. . . . I knew what I wanted to do: get this band together. I was becoming this very unlikely missionary for a new kind of music. That's what Jimmy Reed, Chuck Berry, Muddy Waters, and Howlin' Wolf did to me. Elvis, Buddy, Eddie Cochran, Jerry Lee, Little Richard, Bo Diddley—it's what all those cats did to me. I'm only eighteen, and already people ain't hearin' this music anymore, and it had lit my life up! Now one way or another I got to keep the flame alive! We were disciples."

By the time the Rolling Stones embarked on their 1969 US tour, their first since 1966, the sixties were in full flood. The Stones were the last active performers of the Big Three (Dylan, the Beatles, the Stones). The Beatles were squabbling and would soon break up. Bob Dylan had injured himself in a motorcycle accident and was now reclusive. The Rolling Stones tour, about to begin, would be the biggest tour rock music had ever seen. We banded together in Los Angeles in September 1969 and started to prepare. Join us.

The Rolling Stones tour, about to begin, would be the biggest tour rock music had ever seen. We banded together in Los Angeles in September 1969 and started to prepare.

PART I: LOOKING BACK

"Nobody was taking the band seriously except Brian, who was deadly serious."

KEITH RICHARDS

An Accidental Photographer

Forty years later, what I remember clearly is running into the pitch-blackness, up the side of a hill, until suddenly halted by a chain-link fence. Behind me a man had been stabbed to death, though I didn't know it yet. I remember it being quiet, though it couldn't have been, since the Rolling Stones were still onstage playing to 300,000 people. Maybe it was my heart pounding or the adrenaline. All I wanted was to get out of there, away from the chaos and the Hells Angels. So I dropped off the top of the truck immediately behind the stage (where the Hells Angels had deposited me) and ran off into the blackness to where I hoped the helicopter that brought me to this desolate place would still be waiting.

I shoved at the chain-link fence. Nothing. I dropped to my knees and yanked up on the bottom as hard as I could. It gave a little and a gap opened. I slithered under on my back but got stuck when my camera bag snagged on a stray link. I wrestled the bag off me until I could get my body through. Then I reached back, unsnarled it, and climbed up to the crest of the hill.

At the top I saw the helicopter across the cement of the Altamont Speedway. I ran over to it and clambered in. Inside was a frightened-looking Jo Bergman. Small, pretty, and with a large nimbus of dark hair framing her delicate features, Jo was the head of the Stones office in London. Huddled next to her was the beautiful, tall, and blond Astrid Lundstrom, Bill Wyman's Swedish girlfriend. They both sat in silence and looked out into the dark. Their eyes in the half-light from the helicopter's instruments were wide with apprehension.

Catching my breath, I nodded to them. Nobody said anything. All during her time at the Altamont concert Jo had been isolated in the tent behind the stage, not even bothering to go out and see the Stones. The general vibe was disconcerting enough, but Jo had the distinct feeling she'd been dosed with a rogue chemical at some point in the day. Astrid had ventured out of the tent only to come back and report beatings in the crowd and chaos on the stage. As the violence escalated, both women had been told to get themselves somewhere safe. The helicopter seemed a good bet. It, at least, could leave. Now they were just sitting there, waiting for it all to be over. Somewhere in the dark a hysterical woman was screaming, "Is he dead? Is he dead?"

Alert and silent, we just waited until the Stones could be heard bringing the free concert at Altamont, their Woodstock West, to a lurching close. Within two minutes the Rolling Stones and others arrived. Running. They piled into the chopper until all the seats were full, and then people sat on top of each other. Sam Cutler, the Stones' road manager—intense, sleepless, and with the dead man's blood caked on his sweater—yelled at the helicopter pilot, "Get us the fuck out of here!"

Keith Richards, smokin'.

The engines revved and the rotors spun up to a blur. The craft vibrated. It didn't lift. The pilot cranked the engines up to a higher pitch and tried again. The chopper rose a few feet but then came bouncing back onto the ground. *How weird,* I thought, but nothing else. I didn't know about overloading a helicopter, or that we had four or five more people in the helicopter than it was certified safe to transport.

The pilot gunned the engines to their limit, tilted the chopper slightly, and, taking off more like a plane than a helicopter, slowly lumbered into the air. We climbed just high enough to clear some low hills, flew a short time, and landed heavily at Livermore airport.

People stumbled and staggered out onto the tarmac and then jumped into a small fleet of waiting cars and limos. The Stones themselves were still moving rapidly, as they always had during the entire tour, leaping into cars, sometimes limos, even when there seemed to be no particular need for it. Turning to no one in particular, Keith called out for his coat, which he'd left behind at the concert. For once everybody ignored him, piled into the waiting cars, and roared off for the Bay Bridge and San Francisco. It was like watching a bunch of people escape from prison.

Mick Taylor

We drove forty minutes back to our rich man's hotel atop of San Francisco's Nob Hill. By the time I arrived the Stones had already retreated to their rooms. I went to mine, climbed between crisp white sheets, and, more emotionally exhausted than tired, fell asleep. As I drifted off, I thought it must be some ungodly hour in the morning. I glanced at the clock radio by the bed. It was really only nine in the evening.

I slept straight through until eight the next morning. When I got down to the lobby for coffee everyone from the Rolling Stones 1969 Tour of America was gone except Sam Cutler and me. Cutler was crashed, exhausted, and still wearing his bloody sweater. Later that day, fearing the recriminations that he knew were coming after the disaster at Altamont, he crawled out the window of his room and down the fire escape to leave no trace at the hotel. Then he retreated across the Golden Gate Bridge to the Marin County home of Mickey Hart, the drummer for the Grateful Dead, so that he could see what or who might be coming for him.

My family lived in the city, so I just moved to my parents' apartment near the Presidio for a few days and prepared to return to my flat in London. I'd grown nostalgic for America after a few years in England and had come home some months earlier for a visit.

EVEN THOUGH I WAS RAISED IN CALIFORNIA, London was where I lived at the end of the sixties, having settled there after a summer vacation in Europe in late 1967. Once set up in London, I had little interest in returning to an America that was convulsed with racial violence and the bitter divisions over the Vietnam War. It was in London that I'd become not just a photographer but one of a strange subset that didn't really exist at the time: a rock photographer. And even then, I'd become one purely by accident.

I'd originally gone to London with no particular ambitions, not even knowing that I'd stay. But with-

in a year of my arrival I had become, via a strange serendipity, a photographer for a roster that was soon to include the Rolling Stones, the Beatles, the Who, and many others. This extraordinary turn of events had begun completely by chance while I was living in a one-bedroom flat and volunteering in a hospital with autistic children while trying to be a writer. Then a friend introduced me to one of his friends, Jon Cott, who was a writer for a fledgling American magazine named *Rolling Stone*. After seeing a few of my photographs, he told me he was about to interview Mick Jagger. He asked me if I wanted to photograph Mick for the inside and the cover. Everything that mattered in the early sixties seemed to be driven by music, and I was as big a fan as any. I didn't think once about it. "Sure," I said.

The upshot was that both *Rolling Stone* magazine and the Rolling Stones liked the pictures. Next I was asked if I wanted to photograph John Lennon. And then one morning I was assigned to photograph Brian Jones.

With some fanfare, Brian had just bought the country home of A. A. Milne, the creator of Christopher Robin and Winnie-the-Pooh. It seemed somehow perfect that this blond rock and roller should have inherited the house of Pooh. And that was where the photo shoot was to take place.

Mick Jagger (photographed
while still shooting *Performance*).
Opposite: Brian Jones, rehearsing.

Bill Wyman.
Opposite: Brian Jones and Charlie Watts.

The House at Pooh Crossing

Brian, playing with his dog.
Opposite: Kicking the statue of
Christopher Robin.

The first time I remember seeing Brian Jones, I was an art student at the University of California. Brian was staring at me from a Rolling Stones album cover. Like the rest of the Stones, Jones seemed somber to the point of sullen, even as his blond pageboy haircut made him stand out. At the beginning of the band's rise to stardom it was Brian who grabbed all the attention.

I discovered the Stones in the 1960s when those years had not yet become "the sixties," even as the Stones were one of the main forces driving youth toward that moment. It was a defining experience for me when—in a sweltering darkroom on a hot summer's night—the voice of Bob Dylan came cascading out of the little radio, backed by drums and electric guitar, singing, "How does it feeeeeeel?" Though I couldn't have articulated it at the time, it was more than the music that moved me. The rise of the singer-songwriter was driving the massive change that was going on all around me. These songs weren't the words of a lyricist put to the melody of a musician. These were the words of the artists, spoken to us. Suddenly—no one knows exactly when—it seemed that everyone was getting high, that these musicians were talking not only to us but to each other, and that we were all somehow in this together. The impression became an undeniable fact. Like the rest of my generation, I was sucked in. It was the best thing going.

The writer Michael Lydon, who would join us on the 1969 tour, said decades later, "What I remember most distinctly about that time were the number of ideas and insights moving rapidly and brilliantly in the music until they became part of an international conversation about life, art, music, and politics. Jerry Garcia was as smart as anybody, as smart as a guy from Yale, who was a clerk for a Supreme Court judge. No, Garcia was smarter, more happening. That's really what created the opportunity for *Rolling Stone* magazine. I knew Jann Wenner among the young journalists in San Francisco, and he asked me to be *Rolling Stone*'s first managing editor. The magazine caught on very fast because Jann had grasped the new vibration just when the old vibration was fading."

For me, rock and roll started earlier. It began, to my parents' distress, with Elvis Presley. Through him I discovered Chuck Berry, Little Richard, and the Everly Brothers. When I was eleven years old I tried to imitate them. I sported a shiny pompadour so slick that while slathered with butch wax I dove into a swimming pool and emerged out the other side with barely a hair out of place.

NOW, IN THE EARLY SPRING OF 1969, the pompadour was gone and the hair was much longer. I drove between tall English hedgerows flanked by forests, in a scene of perfect tranquility. I turned

It was as if Brian had chosen to become the Crown Prince of Stonedness.

into a drive and saw a three-story brick house. I went in, stooping slightly under the low door, and saw Brian shambling sleepily downstairs. It was the early afternoon.

He talked quietly, telling me about his new house. He showed me around the downstairs, proud of its Winnie-the-Pooh provenance and the views from the mullioned windows of the English gardens.

Brian, more than any of his contemporaries, seemed to have invented the rock-and-roll lifestyle. It was as if he had chosen to become the Crown Prince of Stonedness. This role required that Jones remain constantly high. Few would have disputed his position, even in California in the 1960s, where people were now setting daily records of higher and higher, just trying to catch up. It was Brian's face, after all, squinting back at you from the cover of *Big Hits (High Tide and Green Grass)*. It was his face peering out of the mist on the cover of *Between the Buttons*, announcing with his wicked leer that he was so high it was a miracle the camera could capture him at all.

A musical wunderkind—friends said he could learn any musical instrument in half an hour—it was

Brian who decided, in June 1967, to attend the Monterey Pop Festival (though he would not perform there). He arrived as the self-selected ambassador from the English Court of Rock to excitement and deference. Pictures of him at the festival show him wearing a long cape, its edges lined with fur, and festooned with a collection of pendants and Moroccan jewelry draped around his neck, his long, blond Prince Valiant hair framing his pale face. There, too, Jones had that Cheshire Cat look on his face, smiling as if he were about to fade away.

But up close on that afternoon in his home, apart from his golden hairdo, Brian looked surprisingly old. He had bags below his eyes, and his face was swollen.

Brian talked rapidly, though in a quiet voice. There was a charm to it; an uncensored stream of stoned consciousness like you might have expected from Jack Kerouac's *On the Road* character Dean Moriarty.

As we moved about his house, I started taking pictures in a vague sort of "Stone at Home" manner. I had him sit by the window in the afternoon light. I clicked away, but I could tell the pictures had no punch to them, so I was at a bit of a loss.

Perhaps sensing my disappointment, Brian said, "Wait here. I'll be right back." Then he disappeared upstairs. About ten minutes later he clattered back down, dressed in a shirt fashioned from an American flag.

We headed out across his lawn toward the swimming pool, Jones striding in the lead. He began to move through a series of poses that he made up as he went along. He strutted and preened. He grimaced and grinned. He snuck up on the statue of Christopher Robin and grabbed it by the neck, strangling the icon of British childhood. I was taking pictures and reloading the camera as fast as I could.

Then he ducked inside a shed for a moment and reemerged holding a gun. (This was not, I hasten to add, some Clint Eastwood, Dirty Harry, .357 Magnum shit-kicker. It was a pellet gun, a rifle used by the landed gentry to kill the occasional trespassing squirrel.) Jones pointed it at the Christopher Robin statue and pulled the trigger. Then reversed it and started thrusting it butt-first at me behind the camera. I gamely clicked away. Next he lay down on the ground, put the stock to his shoulder, and aimed the rifle directly at me.

I was confused about how this quiet fellow, who had a few minutes ago been speaking in hushed and reverent tones about the history of his house and the wonder of Winnie-the-Pooh, came to be writhing in the dirt in his garden attacking everything around him with a gun. Still, I thought, *This is great! Here's a Rolling Stone doing, well, Rolling Stone things!* The images I was getting were stoned and rebellious, with a slight edge of violence. This was the stuff.

When we were done with the session, Brian, polite and quiet again, saw me off. As I pulled out of the drive I caught a glimpse of him in the rearview mirror. Brian stood, framed by his green lawns and his quaint brick cottage, decked out in his American-flag shirt with his rifle tucked under his arm, waving farewell.

Opposite: Brian, strangling Christopher Robin.

Honey, It Ain't No Rock-and-Roll Show

On July 3, 1969, Brian Jones was discovered motionless on the bottom of his swimming pool at Cotchford Farm. Attempts to revive him failed. The coroner's report ruled it "death by misadventure." That drugs were not somehow involved was inconceivable. It was just too easy to imagine the Crown Prince of Stonedness too drunk, pilled, and fucked up one too many times. Even so, news of Brian's death was for me an incomprehensible event. It seemed impossible. We were young. We were special. Everything in music told us so.

Things had been bad for the Rolling Stones for some time, but they had been going much worse for Brian.

"Nineteen sixty-seven was a terrible year for the Stones," said Jo Bergman, the Stones' office manager, whose work at the time kept the whole Stones enterprise *almost* on track. "The raid on Keith's home in Redlands, Mick busted at the airport, Brian busted in his flat. The authorities were trying to make an example of them. It was persecution, really. Even the London *Times*—not, you know, an underground paper—wrote an editorial protesting Mick's arrest, saying it was questionable whether he was being treated like 'any ordinary young man.' The charges against Mick and Keith were finally dropped. But it was all a nightmare. I remember Brian calling me at seven-thirty in the morning saying, 'They're breaking my door down. They're taking me to Chelsea nick. Can you come?'

"Brian was just getting more and more removed from the rest of the band," Jo recalled. "Keith and Anita essentially hid out at Keith's place at Redlands. Mick was in charge, running the office, getting the album made, and trying to figure out what was going to happen in terms of the band's future.

"We were dealing with firing our manager, Allen Klein, and with touring plans, and all of the other things that were about going forward. But what to do about Brian? 'Can we get Brian into America? Is he still going be part of the group? What's going to happen here?' In the background there was always the constant harassment from the police."

IT DIDN'T GET BETTER. In October 1967 Brian Jones had been convicted of drug possession and sentenced to nine months' prison time. He was released pending an appeal. In May 1968, he was arrested again for possessing cannabis. During the same period he'd been hospitalized for strain.

Whether from strain, drugs, or a combination, Jones had become less and less a force within the Stones. Even though he had been the prime mover behind the formation and rise of the Rolling Stones (he'd even come up with the name), his contributions had now dropped off to next to nothing. He couldn't be depended upon to show up at rehearsals and recording sessions.

Bill Wyman said, "There were two Brians . . . one was introverted, shy, sensitive, deep-thinking . . . the other was a preening peacock, gregarious, artistic, desperately needing assurance from his

The crowd at Hyde Park. The "Concerts in the Park" series was organized by Blackhill Enterprises, inspired in part by the free concerts that were happening in America. The Stones' appearance—actually the sixth in the series—would be the biggest up until that point, and would hold that record briefly until it was swept away by Woodstock in just over a month.

"I can't remember the timing, at what point Brian was out and Mick Taylor was in. It didn't start as a memorial. It became one." GEORGIA BERGMAN

Mick Taylor remembers their first rehearsal as "really ragged. I thought, how do these guys make such great records when they're so sloppy and spontaneous? But it was because they had this great chemistry."

peers. He pushed every friendship to the limit and way beyond." Although they'd become famous through their bad-boys image, the Rolling Stones had never been fond of just drifting along. They were a hardworking band, and Brian, more and more, seemed incapable of carrying his share. Something had to be done.

In what must have been an uneasy meeting, Mick, Keith, and Charlie drove to Brian's home in June 1969 to tell him that he was out of the band. Initially, Brian didn't seem to care all that much. He was, from all reports, happy enough.

The Stones needed to find a replacement and quickly selected Mick Taylor, a dedicated, extremely talented, and hardworking guitarist. In order to introduce the new Rolling Stones, the band decided to give a free concert in London's Hyde Park.

A few days prior to the Hyde Park concert, Brian called Shirley Arnold, the founding member of their fan club and now an old, dear member of the Rolling Stones office. He asked her what she thought of the idea that he might go to the Hyde Park concert. Shirley said she thought it would be fine, a lovely idea. And it seemed to Shirley that he planned to attend. But two days before the concert, he was dead.

His passing stunned his friends and his fans and the Stones. But there was never an instant when the concert at Hyde Park was not going to go ahead. It just shifted focus from a celebration to a celebration/memorial. "It didn't start as a memorial," said Jo. "It became one."

I was with Mick Jagger on the morning of the concert as he was filmed for an interview with Granada television. He was sick, taking prescription medication for his voice. Some speculated it was the Mick Jagger version of stage fright. The trials and tribulations of the preceding years had taken their toll. Adding to the tension was the fact that the Rolling Stones had not performed in front of a significant audience for years. Mick Taylor remembers their first rehearsal as "really ragged. I thought, how do these guys make such great records when they're so sloppy and spontaneous? But it was because they had this great *chemistry*." Now they were about to play before a quarter of a million people in the park.

Inside the hotel room before the show, people milled about. The Granada film crew was there, and, of course, I was there taking the odd picture. Keith lay on a couch next to Michael Cooper, the legendary photographer of the Beatles' *Sgt. Pepper* cover and the Stones' *Their Satanic Majesties Request*. Mick Taylor recalls, "Before the concert, the feeling in the hotel room was intense, this sense of pressure on all of us and this feeling of loss." As the time to perform approached, you could feel the atmosphere of dread and expectation thicken in the room.

The luminous Astrid Lundstrom, then Bill Wyman's long-term girlfriend, remembers the mood: "It felt like we were in a bubble, like all of us were separate from the rest of the world; like something had happened to us that hadn't happened to anyone else. Everyone felt shell-shocked, and now they had to go out and do this huge concert. It was quite an effort, I think, to do that. Maybe it's just how it affected me, but it felt like—closeness is not quite what I mean—it had a certain strangeness because of Brian's death. It was a lot of darkness, really, coupled with this 'the show must go on' kind of thing."

We went downstairs, where the Stones climbed into an armored van. I followed the van into the park in a convertible. As we drove into Hyde Park, the tall trees let the summer sun glimmer through. Then the scene began to vibrate and get just a little bit liquid around the edges. I suddenly felt stoned. It dawned on me that the brownies offered to Jagger at the Granada interview (which he had wisely declined) had been spiked with hashish. I'd eaten two. I looked out at the crowd—thin at first, and then increasing to an ocean of people through which we drove. They parted in front of us like a school of fish in front of a scuba diver.

It was a beautiful day in Hyde Park. The crowd stretched away in all directions, filling every space from the top of a broad shallow hill to its base, where the high stage had been set up. I wandered along the edges of the crowd, taking pictures. It was a peaceful mob on a peaceful afternoon in a peaceable kingdom. I could see scattered signs, usually sporting the peace symbol, and signs that echoed the sentiments of "revolution"—feelings that were emanating from war-torn America and had been imported to England in short order. England, though, wasn't at war, and the napalm, the bombs, and the guns of that July in Vietnam were a very long way away from that pastoral afternoon.

The year before, Jagger and Richards had released "Street Fighting Man," a song that became an instant anthem for the antiwar movement. But "Street Fighting Man," like so many Stones songs, is clearly ambiguous in its message. Yes, the world is burning, but London is a sleepy town. What can a poor English boy do?

> *Hey! Think the time is right for a palace revolution*
> *But where I live the game to play is compromise solution*

Americans were more likely to hear "palace revolution" than "compromise solution." Even if they heard it, they were certain the Stones were about revolution. In the politically charged streets of the USA, people weren't making any subtle distinctions.

Underneath the stage in Hyde Park, Tom Keylock, once Brian Jones's chauffeur and now Keith Richards's, instructed a group of British "Hells Angels" about security. I looked at them. They were kids. Some looked twelve years old, maybe fourteen, and it occurred to me that they might well go home to their parents. Some were just generic bikers. Some were wearing wigs for the look. Others sported Nazi paraphernalia. I was from California, so it was easy for me to tell that these were no Hells Angels. Not one of them was the real deal. But I think that the Stones really didn't know and maybe thought that if they weren't exactly like their American counterparts, they were similar enough. Or, more likely, the Stones didn't think about it at all. Their casual impression that these kids were somehow like real Hells Angels would have disastrous consequences months later.

The use of the Hells Angels as "security" at concerts and other countercultural events in the late sixties was a San Francisco phenomenon. The Angels were first brought into the hippie scene as part of Ken Kesey's acid-trip festivals at his home in La Honda in the Santa Cruz Mountains. And in that scene, if Kesey said they were cool, then they were. Later they were assimilated into the San

Mick Jagger leaps as hundreds of small white butterflies are released in tribute to Brian Jones's passing. *"Peace, peace! he is not dead"* read Mick from Shelley, and the Rolling Stones played on.

Assorted English "bikers" at Hyde Park.

Francisco Haight-Ashbury hippie scene. These Hyde Park "Hells Angels" were a parody of the California biker gang. They were all style and no edge.

The crowd roared as Mick Jagger, dressed in a white smock, his hair still darkened from his role in the movie *Performance*, came onstage with the rest of the band. The people were ready to rock, but Mick had something to do first. He raised his hands and asked several times for quiet. The crowd settled down. Then Mick picked up a slim volume and read from Shelley's poem *Adonais* as thousands of white butterflies were released:

> Peace, peace! he is not dead, he doth not sleep—
> He hath awaken'd from the dream of life—
> 'Tis we, who lost in stormy visions, keep
> With phantoms an unprofitable strife,
> And in mad trance, strike with our spirit's knife
> Invulnerable nothings.—We decay
> Like corpses in a charnel; fear and grief
> Convulse us and consume us day by day,
> And cold hopes swarm like worms within our living clay.

With that the Rolling Stones said farewell to Brian Jones and stumbled into "I'm Yours, She's Mine." Bill Wyman remembered: "It was such a fabulous day. It all went like a dream except we were out of tune. Couldn't help that because we tuned up in one of the air-conditioned caravans, and the only thing we could tune to was a harmonica because we didn't have tuners then. So we all got tuned up to the harmonica, and then we went out into brilliant sunshine, and, of course, it changed all the tuning, so everybody was trying to tune to something. Mick Taylor was trying to tune to Keith, who was out of tune with me, and we were out of tune with the piano."

But once onstage, the Stones pressed on. Finding the groove, they recovered, retuned, and regrouped. The lead and bass guitars merged, the drums slammed in behind, the quick count "one-two" was heard and Jagger belted out, "I was born in a cross-fire hurricane / And I howled at my ma in the driving rain!" And the Stones were back. The vibrations of "Jumpin' Jack Flash" pulled the band together, and the sound of the band drove outward into the crowd of 250,000. Trapped on a tower next to the stage, stoned and unable to move, my pictures were not particularly good. The Stones played a few classics but also a number of songs from their new album. After "Honky Tonk Woman," they continued with "Street Fighting Man." "In sleepy London town, there's just no place for a street fighting man," Mick sang. The crowd on this drowsy and long English summer afternoon seemed to agree.

Within a day of the concert, Jagger flew to Australia to film *Ned Kelly*, accompanied by his girlfriend, Marianne Faithfull, fresh from convent school full-lipped, blond, and beautiful. While in Australia, Marianne, who had once lived with Brian and Anita Pallenberg in London, tried to commit suicide. Legend has it that while looking at herself in the mirror she saw the face of Brian looking back at her. We were living in shaky times, but no one seemed willing to acknowledge it.

These Hyde Park "Hells Angels" were a parody of the California biker gang. They were all style and no edge.

PART II: THE TOUR

Oriole House: The Rolling Stones' LA Dormitory

On August 6, 1969, at John Lennon's country home, I photographed the Beatles in their last photo session together, though I didn't know it at the time. Around then, something in me yearned for America. I had not seen my family for over two years, so I boarded a flight—first class, I believe, to reflect my new wonderfulness—and flew back to San Francisco.

Back in California, it was the height of the sixties, and the hippies were ascendant everywhere. On the radio, the Stones' newest hit, "Honky Tonk Woman," played in heavy rotation. Lots of cowbell and then that Keith Richards raunchy guitar comes in low-down and dirty. "Gimme, gimme, gimme the honky tonk blues." The last time I was listening to the Rolling Stones in California, I was just another fan. But now I knew them, and I had photographed the cover to their hit song.

Somehow I heard that the Rolling Stones were in Los Angeles. Maybe Jo called me, or Glyn Johns. We had all become friends. So I got on a plane and flew down. Following Jo's directions, I turned left off the Sunset Strip onto Doheny Drive, drove up the winding street into the hills, and then right onto Oriole Drive and up to the very top of the hill. I parked in front of the last house on the street that was obscured by a high hedge.

I opened the unlocked gate onto a vast sweep of lawn, went to the closest door, and entered. Inside the Oriole House, as we called it, was a classic example of upscale, LA tacky. It was all view and shag carpet. The house overlooked the endless, gridded panorama of the streets and houses below. The wall facing this vista was covered in mirrors so that it, too, reflected the view. The mirror was composed of smoked glass laced with gilt veins in some forgotten interior designer's demented idea of Roman opulence. In the middle of this reflecting wall sat a gas-jet fireplace, left burning night and day.

The kitchen flowed into the rambling living room where I saw my friends from England, now strangely teleported into this California house. Jo Bergman was, predictably, glued to a telephone, but smiling and waving hello. She hung up. "I can't *stand* it anymore" was the first thing she said. "I think I'm finally going to go *crazy!*"

Stanley Booth, a writer from the American South who was about to start a fifteen-year book project about the Stones, was laying on a sofa in the living room chatting to the dapper and intense Glyn Johns, then and now one of the greatest recording engineers and record producers to come out of England. Pacing in front of the window was Ronnie Schneider, an American I'd seen in England but knew less well. Ronnie was the newly appointed business manager for the Rolling Stones' upcoming tour. He was ebullient and upbeat, crowing about deals he was putting together for the forthcom-

> ## "I remember mostly what a small group it was. Today it's like organizing an army to go into battle. In 1969 it was very small and, in a way, very intimate." MICK TAYLOR

Mick Taylor, Keith Richards, and Sam Cutler at breakfast.

Keith and Mick check the proofs for the album cover of *Let It Bleed*.

Opposite, top: Mick Jagger and Tommy Smothers meeting about the Rolling Stones appearing on the Smothers Brothers show. They chose Ed Sullivan.
Opposite bottom, and this page: Rehearsing at Stephen Stills's house.

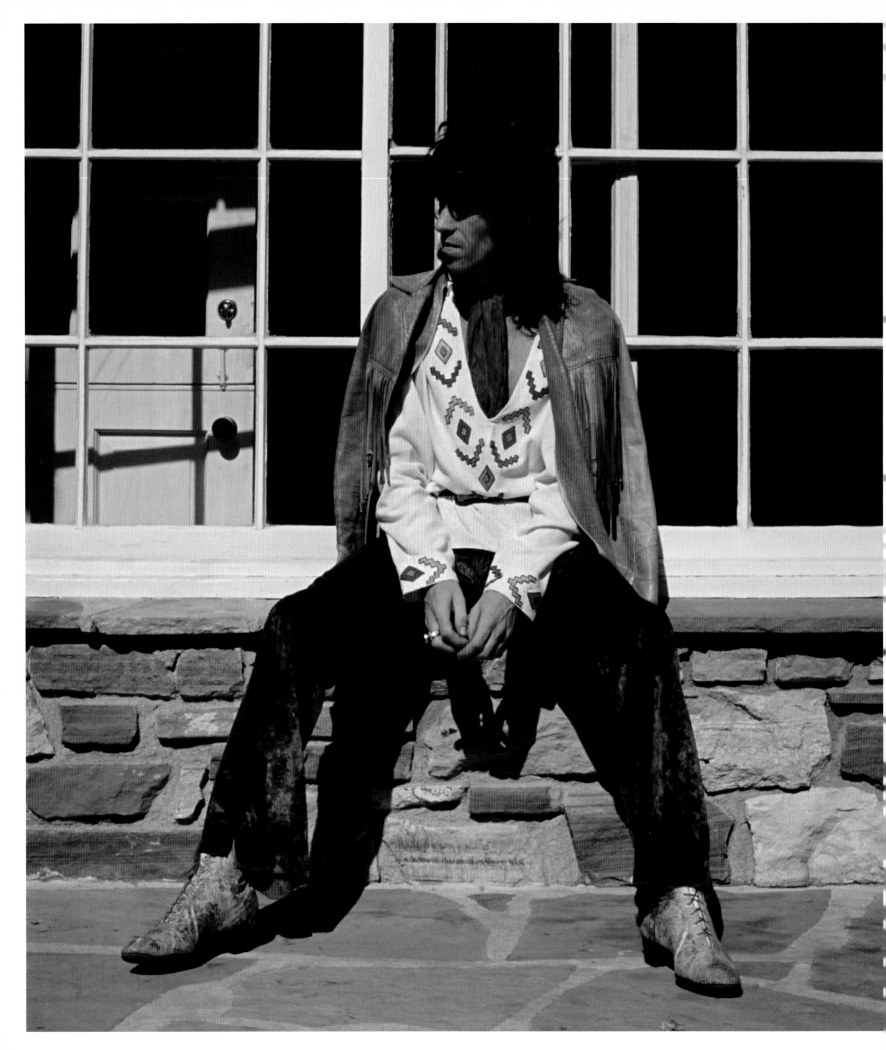

ing tour. Michael Lydon (pale blue jeans, white Indian shirt, and light brown hair to his shoulders) had just arrived from Mendocino to cover the tour for the *New York Times*. He remembers: "Ronnie was very, very funny. So eager, so bright eyed and bushy tailed. Mister 'Get another nickel out of 'em.'" Ronnie was Allen Klein's nephew. Until just a few months earlier, Allen Klein had been the manager for the Rolling Stones. Then he'd been fired. Klein did not take that well and refused to accept it. At the same time he also refused to give the Stones any of the large amounts of money he was holding in their name. Since Ronnie had worked for his uncle before the Stones fired him, it was only irrational that the Stones should hire Ronnie in his uncle's stead.

THE STONES WERE INTENT ON STEPPING OUT ON THEIR OWN, and Ronnie was who they knew, since he had done the 1966 Stones tour with Allen Klein. Years later Ronnie explained to me just how hand-to-mouth the tour was:

> Mick called from the set of *Ned Kelly* about three in the morning and says, "We want you to do the tour." So I said, "Look, I'd love to do it but you're going to have to get my uncle's permission. I don't want to cause problems with anybody." My uncle had begun to arrange the tour but I took over, saying, "I'll do it. It's me." He'd started a deal with the William Morris Agency to be the tour's bookers. I told them no. They came back begging, and I said, "Okay, but we'll only give you five percent instead of ten percent. You just handle all the details I can't."
>
> William Morris said, "Okay, but don't tell anybody that we agreed to five percent."
>
> Mick told me that for this tour the Rolling Stones wanted to do this whole packaging thing. "We're going to put on the show. We're going to have our own acts with us. We're going to pay them, not the local promoter. We're putting on the entire show." So I say, "Fine, but you've also got to pay the guys who are doing the building. Chip Monck and all those guys."
>
> There was one minor problem with all of this, though. We had no money, nothing.
>
> Finally I went to William Morris and I say to them, "Loan us some money to do the tour." They say okay, but I had to sign away my life. I did, and since I didn't have anything I didn't care. Then I said, "I control the contracts. I control everything." And, amazingly, they agreed.
>
> So in the contracts, wherever it said "William Morris," I'd cross that out and write in "Rolling Stones Ltd" which was my company. I needed to get half the money up front—that's the money I would use to pay everyone to get started. Even with that, all William Morris ended up giving me to get the tour off the ground was fifteen grand.
>
> From before the beginning we had to pray that the first five dates happened. Any problem with any of them, and the shit was hitting the fan. I had fifteen thousand dollars up front to finance a half-a-million-dollar tour—to pay for the construction of the set, the stage, the lights, to guarantee the acts, to do everything. It was a very funny moment.

I hung around, talking with Jo and Glyn and looking out through the windows at the hills, homes, and long, flat stretches of LA below. Phones were ringing constantly. In the kitchen a striking, dark-

"I had fifteen thousand dollars up front to finance a half-a-million-dollar tour—to pay for the construction of the set, the stage, the lights, to guarantee the acts, to do everything. It was a very funny moment."

RONNIE SCHNEIDER

haired woman prepared avocado and sprout sandwiches and poured tall glasses of Altadena raw milk.

Within a few hours, Sam Cutler arrived with Mick, Keith, and Mick Taylor. Sam looked like a cross between Captain Hook and Uriah Heep, gaunt and intense. Besides Mick and Keith, Sam was also accompanied by Cathy and Mary, two California women whom he had picked up at the Whisky a Go Go on Sunset Strip and was about to enlist as drivers. Mick and Keith disappeared into a back room to meet with Ronnie.

"Our real serious goal," remembers Cathy, "was to meet Mick Jagger. We were groupies, but not just any groupies. We were among that elite group of seven or eight who could walk into the Whisky and hang out. One night Sam Cutler came up to us—we didn't know who he was—and asked if we wanted to get in the limo in front of the Whisky. There was a guy in there. We asked, 'Is he English?'—you could tell Sam was English as soon as he opened his mouth. Sam said, 'Yeah.' We asked if he was in a group. Sam said, 'Yeah.' So we left with him and scrambled into the waiting limo.

Mick Taylor and Cathy in the Oriole House.

"Inside Mick Taylor was looking all forlorn because these two dopey girls were jumping in the car with him. We didn't recognize him because our recognition of the Stones was from the other guys in magazines. We went up to a place on top of the hill and got out of the car. Sam asked us to make some tea and toast and said the other guys would be there soon.

"We still had no idea what the group was. Then up the driveway came the car with the lights flashing and Keith Richards walked in with his pink sunglasses and his cape. Mick Jagger followed him in his crushed yellow velvet pants and his little frilly girlie shirt and said, 'Could you make us some tea and toast as well?' Mary and I couldn't believe it. I think I still have fingernail marks on my palms from us holding each other's hands."

"A couple of days later," Cathy recalled, "Sam Cutler said Mick kind of fancied me and wished I'd come back. That's when I explained I'd love to hang with them, but I had a daughter to take care of. Sam fired the chauffeur and hired me to drive. He paid me an insane amount of money for that time.

"That's how I became Mick's driver, which was a joke because even to this day I'm the worst, most dyslexic driver. I never know where the hell I am and where I'm going. I remember trying to drive to the airport in Chicago during the tour. I ended up in front of a police department with Keith in the back doing up. He glances out the window and says to Mick, 'You can fuck her, but can we get a different driver?'"

EXCEPT FOR THE CONSTANTLY RINGING PHONES, the atmosphere at Oriole House was low-key and friendly. "I remember mostly what a small group it was," said Mick Taylor. "Touring the Rolling Stones today . . . it's like organizing an army to go into battle. In 1969 it was very small, and in a way, very intimate."

And then later on the afternoon of my arrival Mick Jagger emerged from his meeting with Ronnie and, with Los Angeles spread out behind him through the huge windows, asked me, as though the idea had just occurred to him, if I'd like to join their tour as the photographer.

"We did some rehearsals. We didn't do a lot. You know what the Stones are like. It was mostly party time."

BILL WYMAN

Rehearsing in Stephen Stills's basement.

And so in this casual manner I became part of this gathering group, assembled from all over the globe, in the Los Angeles hills. Our makeup was eclectic. We were from Sweden, London's East End, Boston, the Okefenokee Swamp, East LA, San Francisco, and Miami. We were English, American, Scots, Swedish, and middle-class, privileged, poor, black, idealistic, and criminal. We were such a disparate group, from such geographically separate places, that it would be easy to imagine that our paths would never have crossed. Really, what could have brought us together? The answer—the answer for my generation—was rock and roll.

LIFE IN THE ORIOLE HOUSE FELT LIKE LIFE IN A COLLEGE DORM. We were an intimate group, just hanging out and swapping stories. Besides myself, the people living there included Jo Bergman, Stanley Booth, Ronnie Schneider, Charlie Watts, his wife, Shirley, and their daughter, Serafina. Bill Wyman and Astrid had their own house in Coldwater Canyon, Beverly Hills. Over in Laurel Canyon, on the Valley side, Mick Jagger, Keith Richards, Mick Taylor, and Sam Cutler stayed in Stephen Stills's house, a prototypical Valley home, but with the added advantage of a rehearsal room.

The days at the Stills house were similar to those at the Oriole House, with one notable exception. Since it was where Keith and Mick were staying, they actually had some security. A solid, ex–Air Force, ex-Vietnam boxer and black belt karate expert named Tony Funches was hired to make sure things stayed cool. Tony was large, intimidating, and experienced. At the same time few were immune to the alternate reality that hovered around the Stones.

As Funches tells it, "I'm in the kitchen of the Stones' house real late one night and Keith comes up to me and says, 'How are you doin'?' I say, 'My ass is kind of dragging, to tell the truth.' He says, 'Well, here you go. Have some of this.' He had that gold bamboo thing. And he lays out some. And I go, 'How do we do it?' And Keith goes, 'I'll show ya.' And I was like—Shazam, man! It was an astral flash. It was an eye-opening, pardon the pun, experience. Me and Keith hit it off fuckin' perfectly."

Slowly the central core of the touring group was formed with casual hires like Cathy and Mary. The pace of the preparations for performing picked up. If these didn't move at high speed, they at least managed to move at Stones speed.

Bill Wyman remembers, "We did do some rehearsals. We didn't do a lot. You know what the Stones are like. It was mostly party time. We rehearse for a week or something, and you end up

Opposite: Mick Taylor, Shirley Watts, and Serafina Watts at the Oriole House.

> "Keith comes up to me and says, 'How are you doin'?' I say, 'My ass is kind of dragging, to tell the truth.' He says, 'Well here you go. Have some of this.' He had that gold bamboo thing. And he lays out some."
>
> TONY FUNCHES

doing a couple of hours here because everybody turns up late, or they don't appear at all, or they're off somewhere else. Keith's socializing with the locals, and Keith's getting stoned, and it was always a disaster. It was basically like that. But in the end we pulled it together. We're good like that."

Stanley confirms this: "I remember before this Keith's lying out in the hammock, and Mick says to Phil Kaufman's girlfriend, 'Go tell Keith that we've started.' So she says, 'Keith, they've started.' And Keith says, 'Oh yeah. Tell 'em they're sounding great.' "

But even in the intimate, enclosed environment of the house, every so often someone would show up who made you suddenly aware of the Stones' wider circle of acquaintances.

One afternoon there was a knock on the kitchen door, and I opened it. Standing just outside was a short, stocky, olive-complexioned man wearing a double-breasted pinstriped suit and a wide tie. His hair was jet-black, glistening, combed back above his ears. In his left hand, he held a cigar. In his lapel pocket there was a neatly folded handkerchief. All in all, he seemed an exact replica of one of the gangsters from *The Untouchables*.

"Hi. The name's Pete Bennett. I just came by to see Mick and the boys," he said in a slightly raspy voice that fit the image as perfectly as his suit.

"Ah, could you hold on a minute?" I retreated into the other room and asked if anyone had ever heard of a guy called Pete Bennett.

"Pete," Ronnie shouted. "How ya doing?"

Everybody except me seemed to know Pete Bennett. He was one of Allen Klein's right-hand men. "The best guy in the world to have pushin' records for ya," he modestly said of himself.

When Mick and Keith arrived later, they smiled at this All-American stereotype, but it was all friendly.

"How ya doin', Mick? How's it goin'? Lissen, I'd like to get a picture, if you don't mind." Pete got them to stand still, and I took the picture. Among Pete's claims to fame was his collection of photographs with famous people. He mentioned pictures with Richard Nixon at his inauguration the previous January, and his photo with Elvis. Pete asked for the film. He said he'd take care of it. I don't ever surrender film, but for Pete I made an exception.

Pete was just one of the many sort-of-strange characters who would drop by the house from time to time, but we still had a cloistered feeling there. We were still removed from the mainstream of daily life. Hanging out with the Rolling Stones at their dormitory somehow seemed ordinary after a while. But when we drove down the hill onto the Sunset Strip, we were reminded that it wasn't.

Mick and Keith on the back lawn of the Oriole House. Mick is holding Seraina Watts.

On the set of *They Shoot Horses, Don't They*?
Opposite: Spreading the stage out before hitting the road.

"Keith came into the ballroom set riding a bicycle, holding a sign saying PROPERTY DEPARTMENT. RESERVED PARKING FOR KIRK DOUGLAS. He put the sign in front of Jagger's mike and cycled away." STANLEY BOOTH

Undercover of the Night

Little Richard paced the stage of the Whisky a Go Go on the Sunset Strip. He swelled against the tight confines of his gold lamé suit. A gold cape draped across his shoulders swirled in the spotlight. The heavy pancake makeup on his face started to run. His eyebrows and mustache were carefully plucked and penciled. He worked the crowd hard, lecturing to an all-white audience. "Look at me. Have you ever seen anything so *beautiful?*" Above his coffee-colored face his hair is pomaded and sprayed into a stiff pompadour. "Shit," he says. "Shee-yit!" Mick and Keith watched from the shadows.

"All I hear today," he preached, "is about the Beatles. Beatles. Beatles! Or about the Rolling *Stones!*

"The Rolling Stones? Shit!" yelled Richard, talking very fast. "Why, I taught them *everything they know!*"

A high-pitched yelp escaped his lips. "I give Jimi Hendrix his start!"

Little Richard sat at the piano, slapped and slammed at the keys, and then a stream of words cascaded from his mouth: "Splish-splash-I-was-takin'-a-bath-long-about-a-Saturday-night . . ." He hammered that piano. Pure, early American rock and roll. Little Richard came from Main Street, Macon, Georgia. As he would be the first to tell you, it's a long way from Macon to the Sunset Strip. "Lucille! Please come back where you belong. Lucille! Please come back where you belong . . ."

"*Am I beautiful?*" he screamed to the audience, and then preened across the stage, a black rocking-and-rolling Liberace.

He took it down a notch, but not by much, and yelled, "Okay, they tole me you was out there." His voice dropped some more. "Tonight, we have with us Mick Jagger and Keith Richards from the great Rolling Stones." Then he yelled, "An' I taught 'em *everything they know!*"

Heads turned, trying to find Mick and Keith, but they were well back in the shadows. Silence.

"I know you're out there. Keith. Keith! Mick!" Silence. "Hey, c'mon boys. This here is Little Richard. Tell 'em I taught you everything. Go on." He paced the stage. "Tell 'em I'm beautiful."

"You're beautiful," Keith said, loud enough for Richard to hear.

"You bet I'm beautiful," says Richard.

Now the audience had found them. People started whispering to each other. Soon people would be winding back to the Stones' tables to make contact, maybe hang out, and then it would no longer be Little Richard's show. Mick and Keith sensed this and left quietly. Besides, they had their own show to rehearse—a show whose preparations were becoming more complex and demanding by the day.

"The Rolling Stones? Shit! Why, I taught them *everything they know!*"

LITTLE RICHARD

? HOW LONG WILL THEY LAST ?
COUPLES
REMAINING
HOURS
ELAPSED
DAYS

The Rolling Stones, cracking up, on Oriole Hill.
Opposite: Mick Jagger, about to go onstage.

IN THE BEGINNING, PREPARING FOR THE TOUR in the small cavern-like rehearsal room at Stephen Stills's home was fine for practicing and polishing songs, but it was far too small to allow the Stones to set up their equipment and perform as they would in their forthcoming shows. Calls to friends unearthed an available soundstage on the Warner Bros. production lot that was being used for the filming of *They Shoot Horses, Don't They?* They booked it and shifted the preparations for the tour to it. When they got there, the stage was still being used for the film's central theme, a marathon dance contest from the 1930s. The introduction of the Rolling Stones into a Depression-era backdrop was both surreal and prophetic.

Stanley Booth remembers the scene: "The whole marathon-dance ballroom set, it couldn't have been more appropriate. The sign looming over the set read, 'Hours remaining!' The irony—you could cut it with a knife.

"Keith came into the ballroom set riding a bicycle, holding a sign saying PROPERTY DEPARTMENT. RESERVED PARKING FOR KIRK DOUGLAS. He put the sign in front of Jagger's mike and cycled away. I was up in the rafters with Gram Parsons, who was wearing this big, brown, obviously very expensive shaggy ten-gallon beaver hat. We're smoking this killer weed—it was that rock 'n' roll dope that had that tangy taste to it—got you just underwater, you know—aaaaaaaaaaaaaaagh! We were stoned out of our gourds, and Gram was just smiling and laughing.

"The Stones sounded wonderful. They'd play through the set and didn't do the acoustic numbers because those numbers were so sincere and so passionate. They tried doing them once, but just stopped. Keith said, 'This ain't working,' and Mick said, 'All right, everybody,' and then Mick walked over by the piano, sat down, and started singing 'Tallahassee Lassie.' These were moments of absolute magic."

Slowly at first, but then with an increasing velocity and intensity, the show came together. Mick Taylor integrated smoothly with the rest of the band. The set list was settled, more or less. Chip Monck, the man who had done the production and lighting for Woodstock, came onboard and the lighting was firmed up. The songs slowly tightened until they all sparkled.

As the stepping-off date for the tour approached, life at the Oriole House started to run at a higher tempo. Jo Bergman, who was rarely seen without a telephone cradled against her ear while making endless entries on her pad, said for what was probably the five thousandth time in her career, "I can't take it! Everybody involved in this is crazy." Outside on the lawn, people relaxed, played with dogs and kids, rolled joints, and then headed back to the kitchen, where there was always some food laid out.

And then it was the first week in November. The dorm life at the top of the Hollywood Hills had been an idyll in many ways, but now it began to fade. It was time to take this show on the road.

Nobody ever really knew what the tour was going to be like. A lot had changed in America since 1966, when the Stones were staring out at straight-arrow American boys in crew cuts with their star-smitten Sandra Dee girlfriends. Just how much it had changed we would soon find out. In traditional show-business style, the Stones were opening out of town. Way out of town.

The front row at Fort Collins.

Start Me Up

Fort Collins, CO, November 7, 1969

Winter folded around us early on the chill two-hour drive through the high plains of Colorado east of the Rocky Mountains. It was the only route from the Denver airport to the small college town of Fort Collins. For their first show, the Stones had set up in the university gym. It was a spare setting with two banks of folding chairs set out on waxed hardwood floors. In back of the stage a large American flag dominated the echoing hall under floodlights that scrubbed the color out of everything except the flag. In this stark institutional setting, Chip Monck had his crew set up the stage, lights, and sound system. As everybody was arriving for the sound check that afternoon, a few students huddled back in corners, staring at Mick and the rest of us as if we were space aliens. Mick seemed aware of the eyes upon him, and every so often he'd just do something: jiggle his ass, or smile. But the strange sense of distance between the students and the band persisted. Neither group seemed sure of just what the other was up to.

By showtime that night, the hall was packed. The kids waited through the opening acts, and I went out front to take some shots. As I took them, I became aware that I was looking at a crowd in transition. Over there was the Sandra Dee look and just behind it the Keith Richards look. Toward the front was a group that had just come from an ROTC drill, and behind them I could see people with hair and clothing that marked them as en route to the Haight-Ashbury as soon as they graduated. Everybody was murmuring and straining toward the stage.

The roadies finished checking the equipment. Chip Monck pulled the house lights down and ran the show lights up. Sam Cutler, who performed the same duty at Hyde Park, ambled onstage and delivered the line he would deliver again and again for the rest of the tour: "Ladies and gentlemen, let's welcome . . . the *Greatest Rock 'n' Roll Band in the World!*"

IT SOUNDED GOOD AT THE TIME AND IT WOULD SOUND BETTER later, but Sam didn't mean it in quite the way it sounded. Later he'd remark, "At the beginning of the tour the band was rusty. When I first called them 'the Greatest Rock and Roll Band in the World,' I meant it sarcastically. Mick got upset. He said, 'Hey, man, don't say that. It's over the top.' I said, 'Well either you fucking are or you're not, right?' In a way the slogan just made them work harder right from the start. They knew they weren't going to play for three minutes and be mobbed by eight thousand screaming girls and rushed offstage. They had to play. And they did. That's one thing about the Rolling Stones: they've always worked hard at it."

Bill Wyman remembers Fort Collins fondly: "It was the first gig, a little university town. We weren't as separated from the audience then as we were in later years. No, it was quite different.

The audiences were different, and the whole thing about the music was different.

"In the years since we'd toured before, psychedelia had come in, so you had all the San Francisco bands, the Byrds, the Jefferson Airplane, and all that lot. They were playing a different kind of music, and we were still playing our roots stuff from *Beggars Banquet*. We'd come back from the *Satanic Majesties* album, which was a bit freaky. But we'd gone back to our roots much more, so we were gutsy. We had some really good songs, like 'Midnight Rambler,' 'Honky Tonk Woman,' and 'Jumpin' Jack Flash,' which were great to play, but it wasn't quite what was out there at the time."

Keith Richards wondered, "What are these kids like now? I mean, do they watch TV or are they turning on in the basement? The audience used to be composed of ninety percent chicks twelve and thirteen. My first thought on this tour was, *Where are they now?* The audiences are much more intimate now. They listen more. We can play much better."

Bill Wyman agreed about the sea change in the American audience. "In '69, they listened. It was the first time that the audiences had actually listened to us!"

The Greatest Rock 'n' Roll Band in the World! As Cutler's intro echoed into the rafters, the band raced out as Chip Monck's Super Trooper spots slashed into the darkness. The Stones grabbed up their instruments and launched into their first number with every intention of proving they were indeed the greatest rock and roll band in the world.

> *I was born in a cross-fire hurricane*
> *And I howled at my ma in the driving rain!*

The sound slammed out into the audience and the rush was intense and instantaneous. The audience, from ROTC to Haight, longhair to crew cut, Sandra Dee to Mountain Girl, leapt to its feet, stomping to the beat, cheering. I was taking pictures as fast as I could shoot and reload. It was clear from this college outpost that America was glad to have the Rolling Stones back.

The show screamed on, shaking the gym and rocking the audience back on their heels. After about an hour Mick sang out to this sleepy college town,

> *In sleepy London town*
> *There's just no place for a street fighting man . . .*

And then: "Good night Fort Collins. Thank you!" They were gone to thunderous and fading shouts and applause. The Stones did not do encores.

When we returned to Los Angeles, late, there was a strange man I hadn't seen before handing out keys to brand-new Dodge cars to the Stones. The man's name, for this part of his life at least, was Jon Jaymes. Remembering him today, I always think of a kind of unkempt Pillsbury Doughboy. Shifty and a career con man, though no one knew it then (he was good at playing his part), he attached himself to the tour by telling the Rolling Stones he was from Chrysler, and telling Chrysler he worked for the Rolling Stones. In the end we wouldn't even be sure of his name. But we were on the road now and picking up speed, so who had time to stop and ask questions?

Got Live If You Want It

Los Angeles, CA, November 8, 1969

The Forum vibrated on its foundations, the crowd was absolutely gone, and the Rolling Stones were back in America: blowing it away.

The night after the Fort Collins show, I was in the back of a limousine sitting next to Pete Bennett, that paragon of Chicago-mobster style. We were driving into the Los Angeles Forum for the Stones show that really kicked off the tour, when our car was stopped by a helmeted member of the LAPD. He blocked our entry and refused to let us pass. The driver, frustrated, started to lose his temper. Pointing with his truncheon, the cop responded: "Move it now."

Pete Bennett stepped out of the limo. He asked to see the officer in charge. The cop took one look at Pete and took a step back. Another officer came over and, with a couple of others, huddled with Bennett for a few moments, quietly conferring. I don't know what passed between them, but the barricades were moved and we drove smoothly through, just like in the movies. "Thank you, gentlemen," Pete said, waving from the window as we passed.

In America in 1969 a rather slippery etiquette had evolved around the concept of security at events like a Stones concert. The Stones needed security. For years, they'd been mobbed whenever they'd performed. They wanted security. At the same time, the security couldn't be the police. Chronologically, this was after the 1968 Chicago Democratic convention, where hordes of helmeted police clubbed mobs of demonstrators in the parks, streets, and hotels. Our tour followed years of confrontation between civil rights marchers and police. That's the police in America. In England the police had been either arresting or attempting to arrest the Stones for years. In both cases, the police were the problem, not the solution. "Uniforms are a definite bad scene," said Keith.

As a result, it was written into the Stones' contracts that there would be no uniformed police in front of the stage. But as we pulled up to the backstage entrance to the Forum, there was a squadron of cops, white helmets, black jackets, jodhpurs. Apparently, rock-and-roll contracts meant nothing to the LAPD. Once backstage at the Forum, Tony Funches, the imposing black man who provided security at Stephen Stills's house, was standing in front of the Stones' dressing room door. Making sure that the Stones didn't get hassled at any time on the tour was his job. Effective but low-key, Funches was the kind of security the Stones appreciated.

"THERE WEREN'T A LOT OF OTHER PEOPLE OUT THERE that could do what I was doing," said Tony. "There were the Free Clinic peace-and-love guys at the concerts who would say '*Please* don't climb on the stage' as people just blew past them. Or you had the jocks that detested the concert scene and the hippies to begin with. If they bothered to do anything, they'd just smack people down. Between those two extremes . . . well, there weren't a lot of us. At first it was just me, twenty-four seven." That night at the

Forum, Tony had it covered, buttoned down. The dressing room and the hallways nearby were peaceful.

The Los Angeles performance started late, with the Stones not going on until nearly two in the morning. It didn't seem to matter, because the Stones lived up to their billing as the greatest rock 'n' roll band in the world. The show was, in the hip parlance of the time, a stoned gas. The band was great and the audience beyond enthusiastic. When Jagger called for the house lights to be brought up ("Let me see you out there, LA. You're beautiful."), they came rushing into the aisles and toward the stage, ecstatic.

From where I stood that night, sandwiched between the stage and the crowd, the energy crackling back and forth was palpable. The Stones channeled the spirit of rock and sent it into the audience. The audience redoubled and beamed it back to the Stones. At the height of this show the Stones broke into "Honky Tonk Woman." Then one rocker followed another until the crowd was roaring, surging through the security guards, who wisely let them pass, crushing against the stage, pinning me to it so tightly that I had to raise my cameras above my head, shoot a few frames blind, and slowly squeeze out.

By the time I got clear and backstage again, Jagger and the Stones were riding the energy of the crowd and slamming out the pulsing anthem of "Street Fighting Man." The Forum vibrated on its foundations, the crowd was absolutely gone, and the Rolling Stones were back in America: blowing it away.

Mick Taylor, Charlie Watts, Bill Wyman, and Mick Jagger approach the stage at the Los Angeles Forum.

Banned from being in front of the stage, the LAPD huddles together at an entrance below the Inglewood Forum.

Backstage at the Forum. *Below, left to right:* Mick Taylor, Charlie Watts, Bill Wyman (hidden), Mick Jagger, and Keith Richards (lying down).
Opposite: Gram Parsons (back to camera), Stanley Booth (standing, far right), and, in front, Bukka White. (Stanley Booth describes him as "BB King's older cousin, a convict freed from Parchment Farm because he sang the blues.")

Below, left to right: Glyn Johns, Bukka White, unknown, Keith Richards, Charlie Watts, Mick Jagger, Mick Taylor, Astrid Lundstrom, and (back to camera) Stanley Booth, Gram Parsons. *Opposite:* Cathy and Mary. "All I really wanted to do was hang out with the Rolling Stones, and we got to do it."

"Bukka handed the guitar to Keith, who started playing 'Dust My Broom.' Mick joined him singing a couple of choruses, then they did 'Keys to the Highway.' Bukka listened, his head cocked to one side, and said, 'That's good. These boys is good. Has you ever made any records?'" **STANLEY BOOTH**

"It seems I'm to wear a white tuxedo. It's going to cost them a bloody fortune to have me play with them, and even more if I have to wear a tux. Cash every night. One thousand dollars. Two thousand with the tux." IAN STEWART

Ian Stewart was a founding member of the Rolling Stones, and was later their road manager—he still played piano, both on their records and onstage with them.

"Klein was telling him there must be no uniforms near the stage while the Stones were playing. The fat man nodded in disbelief. 'What happens if twenty thousand kids rush the stage?' 'We'll cross that bridge when we come to it,' said Klein. And the fat man said 'Oh, I see, great.'" STANLEY BOOTH

Below: Sam Cutler points at someone trying to climb onstage.
Opposite: Mick being escorted to the stage by Pete Bennett ("I'm the best guy in the world to have pushin' records for ya") and unknown security.

"What are these kids like now? I mean, do they watch TV, or are they turning on in the basement?"
KEITH RICHARDS

Stoning the Coliseum

Oakland, CA, November 9, 1969

The American conviction that the Stones both meant more and were more than just a rock-and-roll band dogged them throughout the tour. It may be hard to appreciate that today, but it was very much in the air in America then. The beginning of 1969 was when American troop strength in Vietnam reached its peak at 550,000 men. It was when the death toll for Americans in that war reached 30,000. The year before, Martin Luther King had been shot to death on a Memphis motel balcony. Riots broke out in a hundred cities. Two months after the King assassination Robert Kennedy, while running for president, was gunned down in a hotel in Los Angeles. In August, with the smell of tear gas wafting into Chicago's International Amphitheatre from the riots outside, the Democrats nominated Hubert Humphrey. Humphrey lost to Richard Nixon. Nixon promised "peace with honor in Vietnam." Peace of any sort would be five years coming. And the killing went on. And more and more Americans, especially the young, the core of rock fandom, were more and more against it. They expected no less of their heroes.

In Oakland, the day after the LA Forum show and just hours before the Oakland Coliseum, the Stones appeared before a few local reporters. A long-haired journalist was direct about the political expectations. Stanley tells the story. The journalist asked "Why haven't the Stones made any statements concerning the US youth movements, marches, and pitched battles with the police?"

"We take it for granted that people know we're with you," said Keith from behind his sunglasses.

Mick added, "We admire your involvement but we're primarily, um, musicians, and last night, for instance, the crowd in Los Angeles needed to . . . weren't ready to . . . relax. They wanted to be cool and intelligent and it took time to get into the frame of mind where it's just fun. . . . We want them to just get up and dance." It was an answer that must have been puzzling to the assembled journalists.

Later Keith reflected, "I don't think they understand what we're trying to do or what Mick's talking about. On 'Street Fighting Man' we're not saying we want to be in the streets, but we're a rock-and-roll band, just the reverse. These kids in the press conferences want us to do their thing, not ours. Politics is what we're trying to get away from in the first place."

Where the first night in Los Angeles had been smooth, if late, the Oakland show got rough around the edges both onstage and backstage. Right at the start Keith's amp blew up. While Mick and Keith switched to acoustic numbers, the show was salvaged with amps borrowed from the Grateful Dead. Meanwhile, San Francisco's reigning rock impresario, Bill Graham, prowled the front of the stage, more aggravated than usual, berating and pushing at the fans that crowded its edge.

Graham was looking for payback. When the Stones arrived at their dressing room, they found one

"I remember you," Mick said to Graham. "I spoke to you from London. You were rude to me on the telephone. You shouted at me! I simply can't stand people who shout on the telephone. It shows the most appalling manners."

wall decorated with a large photograph of Graham giving then the finger. Somebody took a marker and drew a speech bubble on it saying, "This is where my head is at." Things degenerated from there, but the enmity between Graham and the Stones had started months earlier.

Before the tour had gotten underway, Graham met with Ronnie Schneider in New York City with a carefully prepared presentation of his accomplishments in rock promotion. He asked for the rights to the whole tour, because Graham wanted the Stones tour to be *his*. He behaved almost as if it was his due. At Mick's urging, Ronnie turned Graham down. Ronnie, who liked to kid around, listened to Graham make his presentation and said, "Well, that's great, Bill, but have you ever done anything that's *big?*"

"Graham gets so pissed and upset with me," laughs Ronnie. "Is he mad. And he goes running off to the New York papers and reports our meeting. Crybaby.

"The Stones say I've got to do something to mollify Bill. So we offered him the tour, but at a low percentage and without his name. I said, 'It's not a Bill Graham tour, Bill. It's a Rolling Stones tour.' Still, we gave him Oakland."

Tough and with an ego bigger than the *Titanic*, Graham never took no lightly. In fact, he never took no at all. The bad blood created in New York was to become blood in the water when the tour came, at last, to Oakland. As the concert's warm-up act played, Charlie Watts watched with Sam Cutler as Graham poked at the kids, shoving them away from the stage, and slapping a young girl.

"Charlie then told me to put a stop to it," recalls Sam. "So I approached Graham and told him to stop slapping the girl and get off the stage. So he starts screaming, 'Who the fuck do you think you're talking to? I'm Bill Graham. I'm the promoter, and this is my stage.'

"I said, 'This is the Rolling Stones' stage, shithead' and took a whack at him. I missed and hit him on the shoulder. Then I dropped my head and rammed it into his stomach. I wanted to knock him off the stage. We fought like that for a while, until they managed to separate us."

The tussle migrated backstage and ended with the Stones security facing off against Bill Graham's heavies. Ronnie remembers, "I'm backstage, and suddenly Graham and I get into a screaming fight. Behind me is Keith, and next to Bill is this security guy, and it's a battle. Graham's giving me the finger in the chest. 'You . . . don't . . . know . . . who . . . I . . . am!' he says.

"I say, 'Stop poking me. You're nothing but a bug. I'll squash you.' To make the point, I hit him in the nuts with my briefcase. That's when Keith grabs me by the neck and pulls me into the dressing room. Bill Graham's security guard gets ahold of him, and between them both they pull us apart."

Sam Cutler picks up the tale: "The fight was escalating, with people shoving each other, until Keith reached through the door and yanked me into the dressing room. I wanted Mick to calm Graham down, but he didn't want to get involved until Ronnie told him it was going to explode.

"So Mick placed himself in front of the makeup mirror, and Bill was let in. He was screaming and bellowing, but Mick just sat there, didn't move at all. Finally as Graham was grinding to a halt, Mick fixed him with this withering stare and said, 'Who are you?'

This page: Graham gives the Stones the finger, the Stones cover Graham's face with cream.
Opposite: Mick examines the buffet.

"Bill stammered, says he's the promoter. Mick says, 'You're Bill Graham? Didn't I speak to you once on the telephone?' Bill said yes. Mick gave a little toss of his head and crossed his legs, and sighed. 'I remember you,' he said. 'I spoke to you from London. You were rude to me on the telephone. You shouted at me! I simply can't stand people who shout on the telephone. It shows the most appalling manners.' With that Mick spun around and selected a makeup stick. 'We'll be on in five minutes, Bill, now don't be silly.' And that was that."

The second show went on, not ending until almost four in the morning, with the strains of "Street Fighting Man" ringing through the Coliseum. The crowd, as it did in LA, and as it would for the rest of the tour, rushed to the lip of the stage, exultant. We left in Jon Jaymes's waiting cars, rolled back to the airport, and then flew to LA. We would be back in the Bay Area in under a month, playing to a crowd that was anything but exultant, but we didn't know that then. If we had known what was waiting for us on our return, I suspect, when the tour reached its final stop in Florida, we would have just kept going.

The Rolling Stones at the press conference in Oakland. ("Mick said, We admire your involvement, but we're primarily, um, musicians."—Stanley Booth) *Opposite:* The crowd in Oakland rushes forward, forcing the closed-circuit cameras to be lifted onto the stage.

Below: Aboard the no-heat DC-3 between Dallas and Auburn, Alabama. ("The worst plane ride of my life"—Mick Taylor.)
Middle: Ronnie Schneider distributing cash to Keith on the way into the Circus Circus in Las Vegas.
Opposite: Waiting for a plane, somewhere in America.

Tumblin' Dice: What Happens on the Road, Stays on the Road

Phoenix, AZ, November 11, 1969

"On the public address system a sultry female voice said, 'Gather round the Dingaling Room, where lots of fun is starting to happen with Kay King and the Yum Yum reunion'"
STANLEY BOOTH

By the time we got to Phoenix the tour and the show were settling into a groove. Still, there's always a "Stones factor," as Jo Bergman would say, that makes the Stones' time interesting. When it came time to leave LA for the Phoenix show, the Stones missed the plane.

Glyn Johns, the Stones' recording engineer, remembers what happened that day. "There was some screw-up going to Phoenix; we either missed the flight or there were no airline tickets. Jon Jaymes said don't worry and booked a private jet. It was a 137-seater—a big bloody airplane for sixteen people and a few hangers-on. We fly to Phoenix, do the concert, and on the way back—while we're in the air—Keith says, 'Let's go to Las Vegas.' This is after the gig—it's like one o'clock in the morning."

For my part, I was sitting next to Claudia Linnear, one of Tina Turner's stunning Ikettes, chatting with her and internally assessing my chances, when Mick walked up the aisle, paused by my seat, and smiled over at Claudia. Poof! Claudia was gone, as the plane started its landing approach to Las Vegas. "When we landed in Vegas," says Glyn, "the crew, the air hostesses, the pilot, all of us pile out of the plane and into taxis. We were a ragtag and bobble selection of hangers-on, groupies, weirdos, Ikettes, Ethan and me, the band, and Ronnie Schneider."

Or, as Stanley Booth tells it, "We walked down the strip strung out like Madame Bovary's wedding party. When we got to Circus Circus, Jon Jaymes just greased our way in, asking a Circus Circus host if they'd like the Rolling Stones as guests. 'Certainly,' the casino manager said, 'we'll put their picture on a wall'—even though it quickly became clear that old-line Vegas casino managers in 1969 had no idea who the Rolling Stones were."

Jo Bergman recalls, "In Circus Circus when they announced that the Stones were there, it was just silent. Nothing. Nobody even looked up from the slots, from anything. They just kept pulling the levers and dealing the cards."

Cathy, the world's most dyslexic chauffeur, remembers Mick saying, " 'Cathy, you fancy going to Las Vegas?' So we all dropped a few more black beauties, or whatever those things were called where you could stay up all night. I remember Ronnie having a suitcase of money handcuffed to his wrist. I think we dropped the whole night's take from Phoenix at the baccarat table."

Stanley noticed that on the public address system a sultry female voice said, "Gather round the Dingaling Room, where lots of fun is starting to happen with Kay King and the Yum Yum Reunion." The voice broke the spell. The Stones party regrouped and left Circus Circus followed by a man wearing a tuxedo and carrying a camera. "Stones? Photographs? Which ones?" he pleads, unable to tell us apart.

Opposite, top: After the gig, Keith Richards diverts the plane to Vegas. Everyone piles out, stewardesses included.

"In Circus Circus when they announced that the Stones were there, it was just silent. Nothing. Nobody even looked up from the slots, from anything. They just kept pulling the levers and dealing the cards." GEORGIA BERGMAN

Below: Somewhere on the road.
Opposite: Jaymes "greased our way in." Here seen talking to a Circus Circus manager.

Phoenix marked the end of shows we could commute to, the shows where we could go back to the Oriole House in LA at the end of the gig. After Phoenix we'd hopscotch the country. Dallas, Auburn, Alabama, Chicago, and points everywhere.

BEING ON THE ROAD IS LIKE DRIVING IN THE FOG. All the shapes you see take on a diffuse sameness. You can make out what's near and passing next to you, but there's no context for it. One hotel room looks identical to another. One backstage dressing room is indistinguishable from the next. The stage itself, carted and reassembled by Chip Monck and his crew from one gig to another, is the same.

Each night, Stanley Booth wrote, we went someplace new and strange and yet similar to the place before, to hear the same men play the same songs to kids who all looked the same, and yet each night was different, each night told us more. They all took place in the dark. We lived from dark until dawn. The days were starting to have a uniform strangeness. In three days the Stones played to nearly eighty thousand people.

Being always in transit has its stresses, but for the most part, we were a remarkably compact and congenial group. Even though the Oriole House was behind us, the dormitory feeling of those weeks continued.

Jo Bergman saw the bubble that we lived in from the center. Of the tour she says, "We were all in it together, and it felt cohesive. But once we left LA, we plunged into absolute travel confusion. We never knew exactly when we were actually leaving to go somewhere. If we made to the airport on time we'd take commercial airlines, and if we didn't, we'd hire a plane. You'd always have to be ready to turn on a dime at any instant. Anything on the tour that worked in the way you expected it to work was unusual. Because with the Stones there was always a 'factor.' It might be the 'Keith factor' or the 'Bill factor.' You'd have the plan of what you'd like to happen. Then you'd have a backup plan, and a backup to the backup. Anything could happen when the Stones were involved.

"We were floating in that travel bubble that forms when you're on a tour; where your only reality is clinging to the other people that are in the bubble with you. Your entire universe is this little touring unit. It's your family—your source of energy, your refuge. More than anything you want to stay inside the bubble, because when you're out of it, you've lost your reality. But then there was the music. It was the anchor that kept us all moored to the moment. I loved the music. There was always that thrill of 'Oh my god, they're onstage!' "

Even so, the road grinds you down. The food everywhere is tasteless. Walk into the hotel room and turn on the television. Every television announcer seems to be the same person telling the same story. Down the hall from the room is the ice machine, the Coke machine. Look out the window. American cars fill the parking lot. In the endless Midwest, the landscape, without mountains, with-

Onlookers in middle America.
Opposite: Ronnie offers some Old Charter bourbon to Keith.

out hills, leaves the eye nothing to focus on. Every other day the time zone changes. What time is it? Does it matter? All time leads to showtime. After the rush of the show, you rush back to the hotel. And then get up and do it again.

At the hotel, the locals who managed to find out where the Stones are staying are lurking in the lobby, huddled together, trying to find out what room Mick's in, Keith's in. You ignore them. You especially ignore the groupies. A girl bent on scoring Mick Jagger tends to have a very short attention span.

At some spot on the road a blond had told Schneider that she had a pound of butter in her purse, and she wanted to spread it over Jagger's body and lick it off. As Stanley Booth recounts, Schneider had tried sending her to Sam. "I saw him, he fucked me, he's a pig." She was angry, talking about girls who were with Schneider: "I really hate those chicks. I really do, especially that one. She told a lie about me and if I go down there I'll probably knock the fuck out of her. What about Keith or Charlie or Bill? It doesn't matter, I'm not choosy, I just want one of their bodies and I want it now. I can't wait around forever, I have to go pick up my little boy."

She wasn't the only groupie with this problem. Everyone who worshipped the Stones seemed to feel that they owned a piece of them. What they really owned was what we all owned, the way we heard the Stones' music in our heads. In that way, the people making the tour happen were the same as those who came to listen. It was the music that kept you up, even as the road ground you down.

Sam Cutler follows the rushed exodus offstage that happened every night.

Bobby Folsom, SMU's 4 Letterman.

Below: Charlie Watts bored and Keith Richards stressed.
Opposite, left: In 1969, Mick Jagger did his own makeup.
Far right: Mick Taylor finds Keith's medicine kit.

"Each night," Stanley Booth wrote, "we went someplace new and strange and yet similar to the place before, to hear the same men play the same songs to kids who all looked the same, and yet each night was different, each night told us more. They all took place in the dark. We lived from dark until dawn."

"The '69 tour was the best tour until then, which gets completely overshadowed by what happened at Altamont. **We had Chuck Berry, BB King, Tina Turner, and Terry Reid, a young, upcoming British star. It was a fantastic tour.**"

BILL WYMAN

At the end of the show, Mick would take a basket of rose petals and, twirling, throw it out over the crowd, the petals drifting down like a blessing. Twenty minutes earlier he had been singing, "I'm going to stick this knife right down your throat 'til it hurts!" You couldn't blame people for being a little confused.

A smoke bomb thrown into the orchestra pit in Baltimore.
Opposite: Friendly gestures from the crowd.

"Then a lean, high-cheek-boned brooding-eyed black man came onstage. Wearing his gunfighter's gun, stroking it with obscene expertise, and even Keith's image, the worst image in the room—Indian, pirate, witch, the image that grins at death—reverted to what it was when he first heard Chuck Berry: a little English schoolboy in his uniform and cap."

STANLEY BOOTH

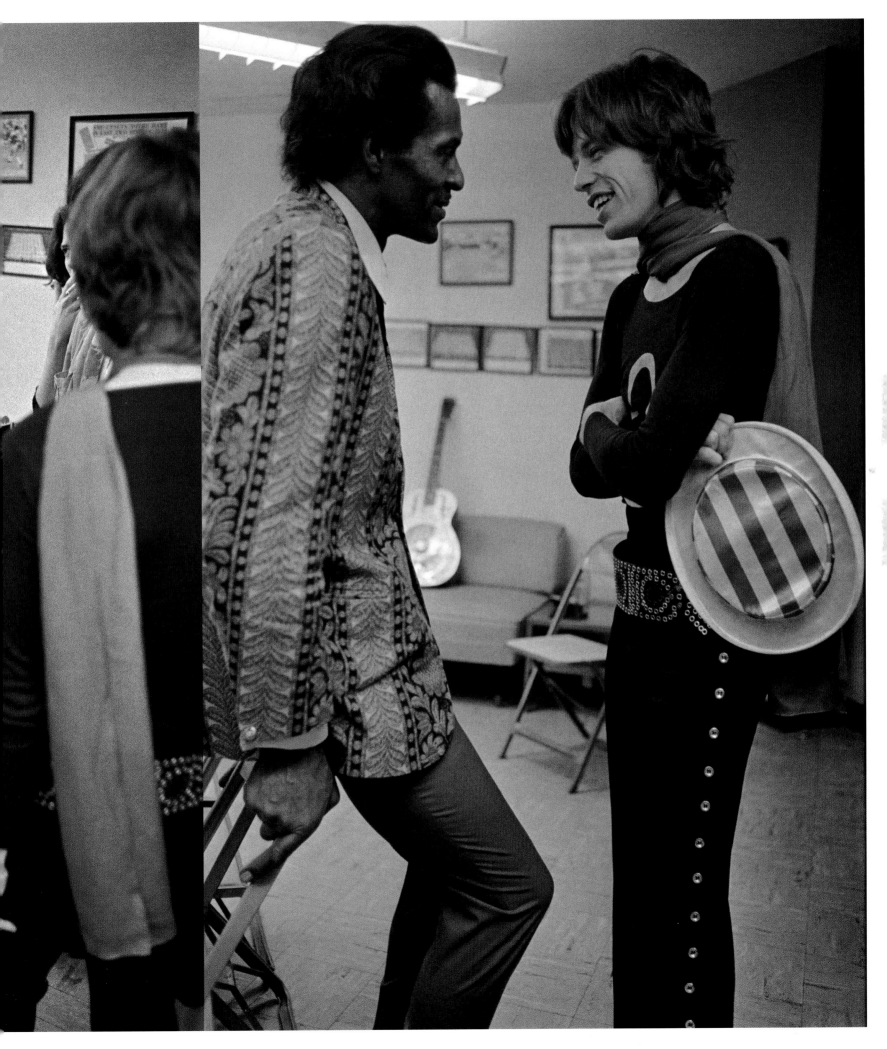

Camera rehearsal for *The Ed Sullivan Show*.

Ed Sullivan indicates he is ready. "All right and taping," says the floor manager. With polished enthusiasm, Ed Sullivan faces the camera and begins one of his famous introductions.

"And tonight, from England, we have with us the Rolling Stones!" He turns toward Mick, who has been waiting patiently. "Hello, Mike," Ed Sullivan says.

You Can't Always Get What You Want

Chicago, IL, November 16, 1969
New York, NY, November 27 & 28, 1969

No matter where we performed, the politics of America dogged us. When we arrived at the Chicago concert, Abbie Hoffman, one of the leading political hippies in America at the time, was there. He didn't have a ticket, but an usher who recognized his face and curly hair let him into the $7.50 section right up front. Hoffman had been trying to get through to the Stones for days. He'd even called the Ambassador West Hotel pretending to be Elvis. ("Yassuh, I jes' wanted to see how Mick an' the boys were doin'.") He didn't get through.

Hoffman sent a note to the Stones from his seat. It did get through and Mick wanted to see him, too. They got together in the dressing room a few minutes before showtime. Mick was dressing and brushing his hair. Both were a little awkward.

They complimented each other on what they'd been doing. "Your thing is sex, mine's violence," says Abbie, and they both cracked up. Abbie asked if Mick knew they were playing at the site of the 1968 Democratic convention.

"Sure I know," said Mick.

"Anita and I just came from the Washington Moratorium," said Abbie. "Great. There was Mitch Miller, or maybe it was Pete Seeger, leading the crowd in 'Give Peace a Chance.' "

"Why not?" said Mick.

"I'll give peace a chance," said Abbie, laughing, "one more chance."

A joint came by and they took a few tokes. Abbie wandered over to Ronnie, who was reading contracts. "Hey, man, you the cat to see about the money?" Ronnie looked up guardedly at this freak in the inner sanctum. "See, we could use some bread for our trial, you know, the Chicago 8. I promise I'll pay you back right after it's over."

"No," said Ronnie with utter unconcern.

Abbie went back to Jagger. "Could you lend us some money for our trial? It's expensive making the revolution."

"We've got our own trials," said Mick. He slipped on his deerskin moccasins. Abbie was left hanging. None of the other Stones seemed to know or care who he was. Mick Taylor asked him for a match.

"Bunch of cultural nationalists," Hoffman said, good-humoredly, as he left.

Starting in Chicago, the feel of America changed. Real cities, with tall buildings and older architecture, replaced the sprawl and unceasing growth of Los Angeles and Phoenix, and the flat, endless landscapes of the Midwest.

Arriving in New York, the casual, bell-bottom feel of California and the "Hello again, Holiday Inn"

banality of the Plains faded away into the formal nineteenth-century opulence of the Plaza Hotel, where we stayed.

In New York, Jon Jaymes, the ghostly man whose presence among us never made sense and about whom there were never any clear answers, was at last on home ground and started to assert himself. His first move was to bring in some big men in suits with cold eyes. Tony Funches, the Stones' personal security man, knew who they were in a heartbeat. They were, he said, "the torpedoes."

Tony recalled: "The torpedoes were good. In Southeast Asia, there were guys that were called LRRPs—for Long Range Reconnaissance Patrol. They'd leave camp with a rifle, ammo, a few survival tools, and be gone for weeks. They'd live off of the land killing Viet Cong. They have a different look in their eye. The torpedoes had that look. They just blended in, unnoticed. But they were always there, always close by."

The torpedoes accompanied the Stones everywhere in New York. They opened limo doors for them while scanning the sidewalk. They stood silent in the dressing room or just outside the door. They walked near them in the street on the way to the press conference at Rockefeller Center, and stood to the side watching the reporters.

Questions drifted across the room: "Do you see yourselves as youth leaders?" "What do you think of the Vietnam War?" "What do you think of America? Do you think it's getting better?"

Then Jagger was asked, inevitably, if he's "satisfied."

"Sexually, yes," he said, and then added, "Financially, unsatisfied."

And then came the most fateful moment of the entire tour.

Weeks before, at the first press conference in Los Angeles, the hippie journalists had asked for a free show. The Stones had not answered in anything other than a vague way. Later, after the Oakland concert, there had been some bad press criticizing the Stones ticket prices, and it had stung Jagger. Then at the New York press conference, the spirit of the recent Woodstock shows entered the room and the free-concert question was asked again. It was never clear if the answer Jagger gave was considered or spontaneous, but he promised then that, yes, the Rolling Stones would give a free concert at the end of the tour—in San Francisco.

"Why are you giving that concert in San Francisco?"

"Because there's a scene there and the climate's nice," Mick answered.

And so the wheels that would take the band to the bleak and tinder-dry hills at Altamont were set in motion, even though, as Mick noted at the time, "There's no exact location yet."

MADISON SQUARE GARDEN ALWAYS APPEARS SLIGHTLY THREATENING, rising up in the middle of a not-the-most-hospitable section of the not-always-friendliest town in the world. The crowd that couldn't get into the show swirled about on the street, ignoring police barricades. Faces loomed out of the dark to peer into my limo looking for the Stones and fell back depressed that they

Ronnie Schneider on the telephone outside the Plaza Hotel, New York.
Opposite: Sam Cutler, Bill Wyman, Mick Jagger, Keith Richards, and Jon Jaymes.

Someone asked, "Are the Rolling Stones going to give a free concert?"

"The free concert will be in San Francisco, but there is no exact location yet," said Mick.

"Why are you giving that concert in San Francisco?"

"Because there's a scene there and the climate's nice," Mick answered.

weren't with me. I felt relieved when we were waved past the barricades and swallowed up by the maze of tunnels that snakes beneath the Garden.

The Stones' security, reinforced by the torpedoes, was pushed to its limits inside the Garden. The pressure to get backstage was unrelenting. By the time the Stones arrived in New York, their presence was felt everywhere. They were praised in the papers and criticized on television. The hard-rock radio stations had their over-amped deejays frothing at the mouth: "The Rolling Stones are in town! Get down! Get down!" The Rolling Stones fans were hyped into a frenzy. At the edge of the Garden stage, by the barricade where the uniformed security guards stood, was where all that promotional energy that said "You've got to have it" slammed into "You can't go back there." The labyrinthine tales concocted by the fans, heightened by the general street rap in New York—where truth is never an obstacle—were spilled before the impassive guards:

"I'm from Mr. Jagger's doctor. I have an emergency prescription . . ."

"These are urgent legal documents. The show cannot start without . . ."

"Listen, you, my father is the attorney general of New York, and when he hears . . ."

The mood could turn ugly when worship collided with force. "All you're gonna get of the Rolling Stones, buddy, is to look at 'em on the stage. Now back to your seat or you won't get that."

"Fucking pig."

"I'm warning you."

"Pigfucker!"

The Rolling Stones never saw this. Back in the dressing rooms, they were tuning up and holding court, entertaining friends. In New York, there was a smattering of stars. Janis Joplin was in the audience. Jimi Hendrix was in the dressing room.

Mick Taylor and I sat on a bench with Jimi Hendrix, who seemed subdued but pleasant, remembers Stanley. I told him about seeing Little Richard in Los Angeles, and he said, smiling as if it cheered him up to think about it, that once when he was with Richard, he and the bass player bought ruffled shirts to wear onstage, and Richard made them change: "I am the beauty! Nobody s'poze to wear ruffles but Richard!"

Mick Taylor handed his guitar to Hendrix and asked him to play. "Oh, I can't," he said. "I have to string it different." Hendrix was left-handed, but he went ahead and played the guitar upside down, wizard that he was.

As Hendrix played, I went into the bathroom to talk to Jagger, who was putting mascara on his lashes. Hendrix had tried to take Marianne Faithfull away from Mick, and he wasn't about to stand around and listen to him play, upside down or sideways. Jagger seemed distracted, but I figured it was because he was about to go onstage. I didn't know that elsewhere in his life a black girl was telling him she was going to have his baby, and a blond girl (who two weeks ago had been threatening to join the tour) was telling him good-bye. Back at the Plaza in a few hours, Jo would write in her notebook, "Tried talk Mick imposs—concert fantastic—Mick better but must keep his mind on necessary things."

"Mick Taylor handed his guitar to Hendrix and asked him to play. 'Oh, I can't,' he said. 'I have to string it different.' Hendrix was left-handed, but he went ahead and played the guitar upside down, wizard that he was." STANLEY BOOTH

At that moment the most necessary thing for Mick to do was to hit the stage with the Stones and rock New York. Stanley again: The people waiting inside Madison Square Garden on this Thanksgiving weekend in 1969 had, most of them, lived through a time of cold war, hot war, race riots, student riots, police riots, assassinations, rapes, murders, trials, and assorted waking nightmares. But if Keith, Mick, Charlie, Bill, and the new guitar player were impersonating the Rolling Stones, and the audience was impersonating their audience, both of them at the moment a great success. Dancing under the circumstances ("Oh, Carol, don't let him steal your heart away / I'm gonna learn to dance if it takes me all night and day") seemed to have a transcendent value. Many people thought then that dancing and music could have a major role in changing the structure of society. They may have been naive, but they were much more interesting than the sensible people who came along later.

Onstage Sam Cutler spoke to the crowd above the high-pitched squeals of amplifier feedback. "Everything seems to be ready . . . Are you ready? . . . We're sorry for the delay . . .

"Is everybody ready for the next band?" he teased.

Tens of thousands of throats screamed out, "Yes!"

"Are you ready, New York? Ready for the biggest band to visit New York in a long time?

"They've done the West Coast, they've done all sorts of other places in America, now they're in New York! Be cool. Have a fantastic time . . . Now . . .

"Let's really hear it . . .

"Let's welcome the *Greatest Rock 'n' Roll Band in the World* . . . The Rolling Stones! THE ROLLING STONES!"

The crowd exploded and leapt out of their seats into the aisles. Security started to lose it. The Stones came racing onstage, snatched up their instruments, and slammed into it. "Jumpin' Jack Flash" seared across Madison Square Garden, and the inevitable gooseflesh rush crept up my spine one more time.

"Oh yeah!" said Mick, as the song ended. "Thank you kindly. I think I busted a button on my trousers. Hope they don't fall down . . . You don't want my trousers to fall down, now, do you, New York?"

"YESSSS!" yelled the crowd.

The Stones played loud and hot, running the gamut of rock and roll for this audience that got everything they laid down and doubled it back at them. They played early American rock 'n' roll ("Carol" by Chuck Berry). They played their arrangement of traditional blues ("Love in Vain" by Robert Johnson). And then they slowly started to kick it up with "Midnight Rambler." The Rolling Stones whipped the audience on, into the night, driving them into a rock frenzy and letting them know, if they had any doubts, that the Original Bad Boys of Rock 'n' Roll, the midnight mover-groovers, were back in town and taking no prisoners.

" 'Paint It, Black,' you devil!" shouted a girl from the audience, requesting an old Stones tune and awarding Mick his dark-demon accolade. But "Paint It, Black" was yesterday's papers for this incar-

Glyn Johns in the recording truck.

nation of the Stones. Instead, the band began and Mick answered the begging girl with, "Please allow me to introduce myself / I'm a man of wealth and taste . . ."

"Sympathy for the Devil" burned the inside of Madison Square Garden with its dark Satanic imagery.

"Pleased to meet you," Mick sang, "Hope you guess my name / But what's puzzling you / Is the nature of my game. . . ."

"I thought Madison Square Garden was going to collapse," says Glyn Johns, their recording engineer and coproducer of the live album. "Madison Square Garden sits well above ground level, on the third floor. In those days, they didn't have remote recording units with everything you'd need, so I flew one in from Wally Heider's in LA because I knew his stuff was good, and set up the control room in a Hertz Rental truck outside underneath the auditorium. I was in the truck, and at one point—probably at the end of the show—I thought there were people stomping on the roof of the truck because the whole bloody truck was bouncing up and down. So I jump out and I look around. But there's nobody on the top of the truck. The whole building, all of Madison Square Garden above me, was moving. I was petrified."

Inside, Mick called for the house lights to be brought up, revealing everyone in Madison Square Garden on their feet dancing and swaying to the music.

"We're gonna do one more and then we gotta go," said Mick with regret, as "Honky Tonk Woman" faded.

Then the perfect guitars of Keith Richards and Mick Taylor started the strong chording that set up an oscillating rhythm almost like a submarine's Klaxon, and Mick singing, "Everywhere I hear the sound of marching, charging feet, boy / 'Cause summer's here and the time is right for fighting in the street, boy."

Bill Wyman's bass played strong descending notes, Keith and Mick kicked it back up again, and Charlie hit the cymbals, bass drum, and snare, pounding to a climax. Keith was crouched, his knees bent, his right arm pumping. Mick Taylor picked single notes, twining through the solid wall of sound the band poured out.

"Yeah!" sang Mick at the top of his voice. "Hey, said my name is called *disturbance* / I'll shout and scream. I'll *kill* the King! I'll rail at all his *servants!*"

On the final chorus, Keith rushed to the mike, joining in, singing, "Well what can a poor boy do? / 'Cept to sing for a rock 'n' roll band?

"No!" yelled Mick. On the last note, Keith flung his arm into the air, Charlie hammered out the closing drum roll, and the Rolling Stones raced off, jogged through the security, down the concrete halls, leapt into the open, waiting doors of the limousines, and were out of the hall before most of the audience realized they'd gone.

"Let's welcome the *Greatest Rock 'n' Roll Band in the World . . .* The Rolling Stones! THE ROLLING STONES!"

Madison Square Garden

"The moment you saw the belt fall you could actually hear the crowd go 'Ahhh!' That's when you know you got it. That's when it's real."

CHIP MONCK, stage designer for the tour, describing the audience reaction during "Midnight Rambler"

Mick Jagger during "Midnight Rambler."

"**Mick Taylor became the most musical person in the band, more technically clever than the rest of us.**"

BILL WYMAN

"**Jagger was grinding his hips, his mouth wide opening a big, orgasmic smile. Hendrix was smiling, as if saying 'This is it—the real rock 'n' roll soup.' I couldn't see anyone who wasn't smiling.**"
STANLEY BOOTH

Coming Down

West Palm Beach, FL, November 30, 1969

"We've lost our business and we've lost a quarter of a million dollars, but it's been worth it because of the kids. The kids are great."

Dave Rupp, promoter of the West Palm Beach concert, whose business was burned and family threatened because of the event

For the final date on the tour, the Stones were the headliners at the First Annual West Palm Beach International Music and Arts Festival, staged at International Raceway in West Palm Beach, Florida. At the site, twenty-five thousand kids—in what was becoming the standard model for these big festivals—waited in the mud and cold, watching Janis Joplin, Johnny Winter, and others. They were really waiting for the Rolling Stones. But President Nixon was in New York for lunch that day, and all air traffic out of the city was being delayed . . . very delayed.

In a small rented plane, we sat on the tarmac at LaGuardia for six hours, a soporific, sullen group. At one point Keith suggested jettisoning the entire idea but was reminded he couldn't, not with all those people waiting in the cold. Keith then suggested that someone fly over the crowd and drop money on it, like Scrooge McDuck. Finally we were cleared to take off, but when we got to West Palm Beach eight hours late, we were taken not to the site but to the Colonnades.

We entered . . . the swankest suite, the Bob Hope, writes Stanley. Caves of ice, glittering polished marble, gilt laced mirrors. It was as tasteful as anything Las Vegas had to offer, and its mirrors had never reflected anything that looked like the group coming in with the Rolling Stones. Past velvet couches, a piano, a bar with drink and food, we found waiting for us in a big bedroom, seeming rather out of place themselves, Dave and Sheila Rupp, the festival promoters. Dave was a compact man in a khaki jumpsuit, and Sheila a small shapely brunette in a splendidly whorish red vinyl raincoat. Dave owned a fast-car shop and Sheila was a schoolteacher. They couldn't have been more gracious, especially considering the Stones were now more than eight hours late. The Stones were the least of the problems the festival had brought into the Rupps' lives.

"Since the festival was announced, my business has been firebombed and burned down," Dave said. "My fire insurance has been cancelled, the John Birch society has been calling me and saying they're going to kill my wife and child." I sat on the bed beside Sheila, whose lipstick matched her raincoat. "The parents call and say that the kids are like they are because they have teachers like me."

"They're right about that," Michael Lydon said.

"That was a compliment," I said.

"Where have you all been?" she asked.

I asked Dave Rupp why he was doing something that was so damaging. He told me he'd once owned a nightclub in Wichita, Kansas, where BB King and Bo Diddley worked and the Kingsmen were the house band. "But this festival is the biggest thing we've ever done. The cops are pigs and the kids are great. I learned that when I was thirteen and outrunning cops in a hot rod. We've lost our business and

"Keith and I stood sharing a joint, and watching one bright blue-white point in the blue-gray corner of the sky. 'The morning star,' Keith said, 'and when she's gone, we'll have the sun.'"

STANLEY BOOTH

we've lost a quarter of a million dollars, but it's been worth it because of the kids. The kids are great."

The Stones didn't go on until almost midnight. When they did get on, the air was freezing and Jagger's breath was visible. Instruments were almost impossible to keep in tune. It didn't matter. The Rolling Stones played until the wee morning hours, until a hairline of red stretched on the eastern horizon, and a quarter-million fans stayed, too, rocking until the last note faded.

THE BIG HELICOPTER IN WHICH WE ARRIVED sat silhouetted against the sky, surrounded by swampy puddles. The entire scene looked like an outtake from the war in Vietnam. We flew out a short way, landed, and were driven to our beachside hotel. We all walked out on the long smooth sands.

On the ground it was darker and still cold, said Stanley, and the colors were not so vivid. Keith and I stood sharing a joint, and watching one bright blue-white point in the blue-gray corner of the sky. "The morning star," Keith said, "and when she's gone we'll have the sun."

Jagger stood slightly apart from everyone, leaning against a lifeguard's chair. "I've got to find a place to live," he said. "Got to think about the future, because obviously I can't do this forever. I mean we're so old. We've been going for eight years, and we can't go on for another eight. I mean if you can do it you will do it, but I just can't, I mean we're so old. Bill's thirty-three."

Keith took an opposing view, "It doesn't matter if you're sixty-eight and bald. If you can do it, there's somebody who can dig it. But if you're a rock 'n' roller, you've got to be on the stage. A rock 'n' roller doesn't exist unless he's on the stage."

Everyone waited for the new, added concert. Were it not for that, the tour would have been over, people would have gone home. Astrid, on this whole tour and on Rolling Stones tours for years to come would say: "I don't think there was ever another tour like the '69 tour. They were playing these huge auditoriums for the first time. It was about the music. There were some of the theatrics that started to appear later, but not much."

And it was almost done. One show to go.

PART III: ALTAMONT

No Problem, We've Done This Hundreds of Times

San Francisco, CA, December 1–5, 1969

> "I told Stu, 'There's all kinds of shit going down here. They've got to move the whole thing.' The Stones didn't know anything about it. They were in a recording studio. Nobody had called them."
>
> GEORGIA BERGMAN

After West Palm Beach we dispersed throughout America, all scheduled to reassemble for the promised free concert in San Francisco. The Rolling Stones went clandestinely to Muscle Shoals, Alabama, to record new tracks. While they were there, they met with Ahmet Ertegun, president of Atlantic Records, who would soon provide them a home and their own label: Rolling Stones Records. Stanley and Tony went with them. Jo Bergman and I flew to San Francisco. Michael Lydon went there separately, but with Sam Cutler.

"I flew from Florida to San Francisco with Sam," remembers Michael Lydon. "He gave me some pill to help me sleep. I remember it created this sort of very pleasant feeling as if the golden sun was shining on my forehead, and I didn't know whether I was asleep or not."

Feeling good and being unclear as to whether or not you were awake or dreaming was an appropriate way to arrive in San Francisco circa 1969. Though the music revolution (or the hippie revolution or the youth movement, whatever you chose to call it) was now worldwide, San Francisco and London were indisputably the two capitals. And in the drug world—smoke a little this, drop a little that—San Francisco had risen higher. After all, Mick had chosen San Francisco "because there's a scene there." Well, there was.

Looking back, Jo Bergman said, "We had a week in between the Florida show and the free concert. I was there but essentially the boys were doing all the work. It was Chip, it was Sam, and it was Ronnie, and the filmmakers, the Maysles brothers, along with the rest of the production team. It was fine by me. I just wanted to shop and have a rest and see my friends."

The so-called Concert in the Park (San Francisco's Golden Gate Park), first broached in London the year before, promoted by Rock Scully of the Grateful Dead, had taken root. (And why not? What a great idea. The Stones in the park!) But Golden Gate Park was not available. The city of San Francisco wouldn't issue permits. No problem. "The man," as was said then, "can't bust our music." An alternative site was quickly selected: Filmways' Sears Point Raceway—thirty-two miles north of San Francisco in Sonoma County. So Chip Monck, who'd set up the stage the entire tour, had gone to Sears Point with his crew and was in the process of putting up the stage. Everything was on schedule, even relaxed. But everything was not to be. The executives of Filmways had their own plans to exploit the profits from the "free" concert.

As Ronnie Schneider tells it, "We had the site at Sears Point. They said 'Free concert, free concert, everything's free.' But when we sat down they [the owner, Dick St. John] said, 'Everything's free but we need you to put up three million dollars for cleaning, three million dollars for insurance,' and they would own the rights to the film. So the 'free' thing was going to cost us six million plus the film. I was

Melvin Belli with Dick Carter, the owner of the Altamont Speedway, standing to his right. Legend has it that Carter heard of the Rolling Stones' need for a venue while taking a marketing class at Stanford. They are talking on the speakerphone and Carter has been asked to calculate how much parking he has. "Enough for eight thousand cars." There's a stunned silence on the other end of the line. The concert was the next day. Hundreds of thousands of people were already on their way.

"We had the site at Sears Point. **They said 'Free concert, free concert, everything's free.'** But when we sat down they said, 'Everything's free but we need you to put up \$3 million for cleaning, \$3 million for insurance,' and they would own the rights to the film. That's when we brought in Melvin Belli."

RONNIE SCHNEIDER

Melvin Belli performing in his office.

totally opposed to this and the deal broke down after everything was all set up. That's when we brought in Melvin Belli."

DURING THE BREAK I stayed at my parents' San Francisco apartment in Pacific Heights near the Presidio. One day the Stones office called about certain hang-ups, but we were back at it, and they asked me to come join them at a meeting in Melvin Belli's office.

It was a chaotic meeting in an office jammed full of film crews and many people I'd never seen. I knew the then sixty-two-year-old Belli by sight. Flamboyant and a raging narcissist, he was a San Francisco legend. If I'd hadn't already been aware of that, it would have been easy enough to tell by the life-sized oil portrait of himself he'd hung above his desk.

As I stood there and watched everything unfold, the radio and television stations had already announced the free concert. Hundreds of thousands of people, from all over the United States, were coming to the Bay Area for the show. But where exactly was the show going to be? Two days before the date there was still no location. And the notoriety of Woodstock had, if anything, amplified the belief among the young that you had to be at the show; it would be a life-changing generational event.

"Altamont was going to be Woodstock West," said Michael Lydon. "Everybody was talking about it."

Things were much more exasperating than exciting for Jo Bergman. "I was lying on the floor with a migraine headache," she said. "I called Stu [Ian Stewart], who was with the Stones recording in Alabama. I told him, 'There's all kinds of shit going down here. These Filmways people wouldn't let them have the concert at Sears Point without all this money, so they've got to move the whole thing. The Dead people are helping.' I basically told him what was going down. The Stones didn't really know anything about the problems. They were in a recording studio. Nobody called them."

I saw Ronnie Schneider in Belli's office, as well as Jon Jaymes, who was sitting glumly in a chair. The television cameras were rolling. I looked over and noticed an unlikely-looking middle-aged man with a pencil-thin mustache standing near Belli, who was holding court in his portentous manner. Belli introduced the man with a flourish as Dick Carter, owner of something called the Altamont Speedway, and the last-minute savior of the free concert. Carter had offered his automobile and motorcycle race-track as the critically needed location. (Years later I heard that Carter, who had just bought the Altamont Speedway, was taking a marketing course at Stanford to figure out what to do to promote his new business when one of his fellow students called and asked him if he knew that the Rolling Stones were looking for a venue.)

The police were on the speakerphone asking about parking. Dick Carter answered something to the effect of "we have these many spaces here and so many spaces there." Someone at police head-quarters was calculating how many people were expected to show up, and there was a long silence on the other end. It didn't require much expertise to know that the crowd would number in the hundreds of thousands. When someone said that Carter didn't have enough parking, Carter blithely answered that he had many neighbors with big fields. The police officer on the other end of the line responded, "They say they are against this concert." Belli blustered and pushed the plan harder. In the end, everybody just shrugged and decided to let it go forward. The new location was so far out of the way, almost no one at the meeting really knew where it was.

After this meeting the concert rushed forward like a juggernaut. The Altamont concert was seen as simply the next logical upward tick of the youth explosion, which had already risen in a steady, ascendant line from the early 1960s to this moment. It had always gotten bigger, always gotten better, always gotten higher. We were stardust. We were golden. And we were going to get ourselves back to the Altamont garden. Here, as at Hyde Park, the show went on.

Dick Carter, owner of the Altamont Speedway, Melvin Belli, Ronnie Schneider, and Jon Jaymes, helping the viewer locate the Speedway.

> ## "But when I get to Altamont I see the place hasn't got any toilets. It's got no fencing. It's wide fuckin' open. We're not in a building. We have no security whatsoever. What are we going to do?"
> CHIP MONCK

As Jo would observe years later, "It was the sixties, dammit. Weird things happened and people did weird things and asked questions later." Think about it: how was something going to appear too far-fetched for San Francisco in the sixties?

The meeting ended. The concerns were deflected. And the harsh reality landed on Chip Monck and his crew, who were given less than two days to move the entire stage, the sound system, and the lights from the relative beauty of the Sonoma hills near the upper reaches of the San Francisco Bay to the desolate brown hills of Altamont, eighty miles away to the southeast. Still, nobody doubted it would get done.

Chip Monck remembers, "When we got to Sears Point, we saw that it was going to be on the top of the hill. And I thought, 'Well, gee, it's a little backwards putting it on the top of a hill, but it's a grand idea. That makes it even easier for us, safer. It's not going to feel as intimate, but it's going to be a lot safer.' We were working at a leisurely pace, when all of a sudden no more Sears Point! With only a couple of days left, nobody knew where the concert was going to be.

"And all I care about," says Monck, "is a location to put something on. Let's find out where it is. Let's find out what it is. Let's look at the pluses and the minuses. Let's lock it down.

"But when I get to Altamont I see the place hasn't got any toilets. It's got no fencing. It's wide fuckin' open. We're not in a building. We have no security whatsoever. What are we going to do?"

Monck walked around the location until he got to one spot that seemed the best of a bunch of bad choices. "Well, I guess we better do it here. It looks like this is the best sightline we're gonna get. Where are you going to want your follow spot towers? There, there, there, and there. You had to move.

"I spent the night before in a truck with a gas heater, which gave me sunburn. When I woke up on the morning of the show, I found the crowd had burned the wooden cases for my big arc lights to keep warm. Three thousand five hundred fucking dollars each! That provided some flavor."

Tony Funches, still charged with the Stones' personal security through this one last show, went out to the location in advance. He remembers, "We got through the official tour with some nuttiness but nothing serious. Not even in the Deep South. Then we went out to San Francisco to organize the free concert. When we went out to the site, there's a pitiful array of trailers for dressing rooms. What I see when I look around is indefensible perimeters. I'm thinking to myself, *These motherfuckers have got to be out of their minds.* My assessment is that it's a complete disaster in the making, so I drop back into fail-safe mode of accomplishing my primary task—making sure that nobody tags the band members. Can't protect the entire entourage. Have to drop back to primary position."

Sam Cutler was hunkered down in offices provided by the Grateful Dead, handling a thousand details. He heard the complaints and concerns and finally flew out to take a look. "The first time I was at the site was the night before the concert, and I stayed there from then on in. One of the biggest things that went wrong at Altamont was that the stage was too low. At Sears Point there was like a ten-foot drop in front of the stage. No one could have gotten onto it. They took that same stage to Altamont and somebody, I don't know who, decided that the stage should be located in the bottom of a bowl, the worst possible location for it. When I got there, I was appalled. But there was nothing to be done about it. We were out of time.

"I'd been up," said Cutler decades later, "I don't remember exactly . . . at least the day before and the night. As soon as I saw Altamont at dawn I knew in my gut it was going to be heavy. It was bitterly cold. There were a lot of drunk and stoned people already stumbling about. Somebody came up to me and told me it was going to be the heaviest day of my life and then gave me a big chunk of opium, which I swallowed. You know, it went from there. The opium was like a gift, and I thought, *I'm gonna need this.*

"There was smoke from campfires shrouding the hillsides, and already well in excess of a couple of hundred thousand people. It looked like there'd been a mushroom cloud over San Francisco and these were the survivors. It looked like the end of the world. But I was in the midst of it. Keith was already there."

For all the concern, the persistent belief that Altamont was going to be the high, extraordinary concert that everyone hoped for was present as late as the evening before. Ronnie Schneider remembers, "The night before the concert was just mystical. There would be three or four of us walking around the land at Altamont and people would come up and follow . . . a quiet procession just following us around. It was so nice and laid-back and beautiful, sitting around the campfire, drinking wine, everybody talking. That's why Keith decided to stay because it was so fantastic. The night before was beautiful: a great prelude to what we all *thought* was going to happen."

Stanley remembers: The night before was like Morocco, but it was also like anything you wanted it to be. It was moving through an imaginary landscape in the dark night of the soul where strange signs might be seen. Keith chose to stay, while Mick and I elected to return to the city for what was left of our night. 'I'm gonna crash,' Mick said at the hotel, taking a sheet of paper from the desk to write Charlie a note about how nice it was at the concert site.

The next morning, still in the hotel, Bill Wyman's girlfriend, Astrid, got a phone call from the site. "They said I should not come out because it was not safe. That is when I personally started to get a little bit apprehensive. But Bill wanted me to come, didn't really believe them. 'No, Astrid is coming.' So out I went. I was pretty much on my own when we got there, because they disappeared into the tent."

The Stones flew out to Altamont in two helicopters. The first helicopter, with Mick Jagger, Mick Taylor, Charlie Watts, and Ronnie, left at about two o'clock. "Have you noticed," Mick Taylor asked before he left, "there's a kind of an atmosphere over the whole city, like a carnival? It's great."

En route to Altamont. Mick Jagger,
Charlie Watts, Mick Taylor, unknown.

Highway 580. The cars are parked.

Altamont: "It's Just a Shot Away"

Altamont Speedway, Livermore, CA, December 6, 1969

The first thing I saw from high up and far out was the shape of the crowd. It was a dark blot smeared on the arid hills, indistinct in the haze. It had a forbidding look in the photographs I would print later, but I had no sense of foreboding as the helicopter descended. I expected, to the extent that I and so many others expected anything at all, that we were on our way to some version of Woodstock West.

I saw the road below us, thought it was a massive traffic jam, and then realized it wasn't lanes of cars creeping along bumper to bumper, but thousands of cars abandoned in the middle of the freeway, a giant parking lot. But that, too, was reminiscent of Woodstock.

As the helicopter began to slow in preparation for landing I noticed that no touchdown area had been designated for us. Random clots of people (some with their animals) were walking across the track where we were about to land. There was no one below us to clear a landing space, to greet us, to tell us where to go.

Once down, I stepped out and moved off the raceway into the adjoining field. It was unfenced, a massive bowl almost filled to the brim with people.

I have noticed in my life that whenever I think I know where I'm going, that's when I get lost. Why bother to check, when you know where you are? And my first instincts are governed by that sense of already knowing what's going on. At Altamont I was looking for the photographs I expected to find there. Happy people. Dancing people. Maybe someone giving birth. Triumphant people. But that was not what I found.

ALTAMONT WAS A DULL, LIFELESS LANDSCAPE, as different from San Francisco as the Siberian steppes are from Paris parks. There was no hint of green at all, not a tree, not a blade of grass. The color was baked brown, the hills parched and arid. There were tie-dyed flags (the emblems of the "tribes") poking above the crowd, and Volkswagen buses parked at its edges. Beyond them, below the Speedway, stood numerous automobile wrecks, carcasses from races held there, icons of another generation's idea of a good time.

There was some dancing, but not much. And it felt rote, like, "This is what we do when we go to a free concert." There was no palpable feeling of joy or even happiness. People were just passing time, getting high, waiting for the Rolling Stones.

I was on the edge of the crowd. The stage, on the far side at the base of the bowl in front of me, was almost invisible except for the speaker towers next to it. I decided to move down toward the

> "It looked like there'd been a mushroom cloud over San Francisco and these were the survivors. It looked like the end of the world."
>
> SAM CUTLER

stage, and as I did, the crowd got more and more compressed. It slowly dawned on me that this concert might not turn out to be what I expected.

Mick Jagger had no such luck. His realization came instantly.

Stanley Booth saw it happen: "Mick got off the first helicopter with Ronnie when a kid comes running up to Mick and says 'I hate you' or something like that and punches Mick right in the mouth. Then Mick disappeared. Ronnie grabbed him and off they went."

Ronnie recalls, "I don't know what the kid said but I remember Mick screaming, 'Don't hurt him, don't hurt him!' Me, I wanted to go kill the guy right away because he took a swing and punched Mick in the mouth just as we were walking in.

"That set the tone. After that, when we got situated, I went back to where we had the helicopter, and I told the pilot that I wanted him ready to get us out of there at any time. But the helicopter pilot gave me this whole story of why he couldn't remain. The FBI guy we had then came over, pulled out his gun, and said, 'You'll stay.' "

Michael Lydon remembers, "You could, you know, wander from campfire to campfire and see people smoking pot and everything. But there were a lot of really weird hippies. There were people who had had weird experiences; there were people who were damaged, or people who had been in prison for drugs. There were girls who were just sort of wandering from guy to guy—talking astrology stuff— that you knew was just unbalanced. People adrift, homeless, spaced, and so ill-educated that they didn't have any defense against culty-type vibes."

Jo Bergman saw it, too. "On the day of the show there were all these ugly people all around. They were ugly from the moment we hit the ground. I don't know if I was around when Mick got hit, but I know that we were holding hands and wading though the crowd from where the helicopter landed to the backstage trailers.

"People at Altamont were lying around, completely wigged out, with other people stepping on them or ignoring them. And they were not happy, cheerful stoned people. They were nasty, mean stoned people. And it was scary. I didn't even see a Hells Angel. Could have been no Hells Angels." But that changed.

"Then I went into that tent with the Hells Angels. These people were very spooky. The whole energy was truly awful. Everyone was exhausted. The people who'd been there all night, the crew . . . all those people? They'd done the completely impossible by having to move that whole stage overnight. Everybody was just far beyond tired."

Slowly, bit by bit, I finally wormed my through the crowd and into the tent behind the stage. The energy inside was tense, jagged. Mick, Charlie, Bill, Keith, and assorted others milled about as Hells Angels watched. Jagger looked apprehensive. At the best of times Mick didn't like being crowded.

As for me, Hells Angels always scared me. I knew, of course, about their new peaceful reputation in the San Francisco scene. I'd read how Ken Kesey invited them to participate, and how they would stand

next to the stage at concerts in San Francisco, a kind of unofficial security presence—an example of the inclusiveness of the new Aquarian world order. Still, I was nervous. It felt uncomfortable.

There was no light in the tent, so if I wanted to take a picture I needed to use flash. I didn't like using flash; it's always too intrusive. Now when I did, I would look up and see an Angel glaring at me. I didn't like that feeling, but I was functioning mostly out of habit. I had the feeling then—it would grow much stronger later—that I already had my Stones 1969 Tour pictures. I'd photographed everything for weeks, so whatever this was going to be, would be extra. I would be glad when it was over.

Stanley writes, Michelle Phillips of the Mamas and the Papas came into the trailer bearing tales of how the Angels were fighting with civilians, women, and each other, bouncing full cans of beer off people's heads. Augustus Owsley Stanley III, the San Francisco psychedelic manufacturer, was giving away LSD, the Angels eating it by handfuls, smearing the excess on their faces. It didn't sound good, but there was no way to do anything about it, nothing to do in the center of the hurricane but ride it out.

Word of more fights and beatings begin to filter back into the tent. During the Jefferson Airplane's set, a Hells Angel had beaten Marty Balin, the lead singer, unconscious. Such an act was unheard of— a complete game changer, as people say today. Musicians were the undisputed royalty of the new age, leading us, note by note, lyric by lyric, into a new world. To knock one out while they were performing was a cultural impossibility, but there it was.

Sam Cutler: "I went and talked to the Angel that had done it. He was short, built like a tank, wearing a Davy Crockett hat. His name was Animal. Trying to be as peaceful as possible, I said, 'Hang on a second. There ain't going to be any music if we start knocking out the singers.'

"Animal said, 'He fucking insulted my people.'

" 'Well, yeah, he probably he did,' I agreed. 'But can we try and get this sorted? Let's get some music happening.' He was prepared to go and make up with Marty. So we went to talk to him, and Marty went apeshit again and started saying fuck you, blah, blah, blah. So the guy knocked Marty out again. At that point I knew, man, I knew, it was going to get really heavy. From then on, it's like memories from the heat of a battle."

Charlie Watts: "The backstage was full of people. A lot of them were fucked up. I was talking to a couple of the Angels when the tent flap wobbled and one of them whacked it with a billiard cue—there was probably some kid's head behind it.

"When it came time for us to go on, the Angels made a razor-sharp line for us to pass through. I felt very worried as we walked to the stage. It was an event waiting to go wrong."

TONY FUNCHES: "SO IT STARTS AND I'M WATCHING IT GO DOWN. There's these two Hells Angels having a fight with each other just before the Airplane went on. I ask 'em to take the fight somewhere else, because they were messing up the stage. They look at me with pinwheel eyes going, and my lizard brain got ready for combat. One guy says, 'I ain't taking no order from no nigger.' I said, 'Oh

"I was talking to a couple of the Angels when the tent flap wobbled and one of them whacked it with a billiard cue—there was probably some kid's head behind it."

CHARLIE WATTS

Opposite: Mick and Keith on the way to the stage.

really? Come on with me, buddy. Let's go around here.' We went back behind the amplifiers. 'So tell me again. What did you say?'

" 'I don't take no orders from no—' Whap! He's out. His buddy gets froggish. Whap! He's out. That's when I broke two bones in my hand.

"After I got a splint, I went over to the cat that I perceived to be the senior ranking Hells Angel guy—the one with the wolf's head. I said, 'I just coldcocked a couple of your bros over there. That makes me a dead man, but I wanted to let you know it wasn't personal. Business is business. They were tearing up the stage. We're trying to do a concert here.' Cat looked me square in the eye and said, 'Man, we ain't got no problem with you. You're just doing your gig.'

Gram Parsons, the musician who had been hanging with the Stones, especially Keith, off and on since Los Angeles, remembered, "Michelle and I were standing by the right-hand side of the stage not bothering anybody, just standing as far away as we could be and still see, and every two minutes one Angel kept trying to push us back. Every two minutes I'd have to explain to him all over again, just like the first time, that we were supposed to be there."

I followed Mick and Keith with my cameras. I hoped that once we were onstage things would return to normal. Covered with people, the stage was actually sagging under the weight of all the bodies on it. Hells Angels were roaming across it at will.

I saw the imperturbable Ian "Stu" Stewart on the other side of the stage. Stu had been with the Rolling Stones since the beginning. In fact, Stu was a Rolling Stone. He'd been in the band before either Bill or Charlie but was asked to leave the group after Andrew Oldham took the reins. It was a sad story but history by the time of this concert. Stu had left the group officially, but he still played with them on records and traveled with them as their equipment man and main man in general. Stu had been with the Stones everywhere, been through everything with them. Stu looked worried, and I had never seen Stu look worried.

Once on the stage I couldn't get any decent pictures. I was blocked by the crowds in one direction and hemmed in by Hells Angels in the other. Fights were breaking out in the crowd.

Sam remembers, "There were fights going on all around me. It was a series of vignettes that were all boringly the same: Big Angel, Small Person. Trying to save the Small Person. Small Person getting clumped. Trying to make sure the Small Person got to a doctor. And on to the next fight. When the Stones were on there were several Angels that looked like they wanted to kill Mick. And I was not equipped to deal with it. I mean, if they wanted to, they could have. Who was there to stop them?"

It was dark now as the Stones set up. Sam called for the stage to be cleared, asking everyone without official reason to be there to get off. Arguably I had official reason to be there, but I didn't care. I was happy to get off. So I stepped back and a Hells Angel, apparently understanding that I was with the Stones, helped me get down and then up onto the top of a truck immediately behind the stage.

Up there I could see the crush of people pressed against the stage, a stage maybe three and a half feet high. People were resting their elbows on it. I could also see plainly that from the stage out to

where the light faded into the night there was *no* room in the crowd, *no* space between people at all.

The lights that created backlight for the Rolling Stones shone onto the upraised faces of people closest to the stage. As the light fell off, the faces faded, becoming indecipherable, part of the compressed mass of blackness stretching out into the night. Suddenly, in the midst of that mass, where there was no space, absolutely no space at all, I saw a circle of bodies open, crazily, like a sea urchin's mouth when a wave rolls over it. That circle would quickly widen until there was an empty circle maybe thirty feet in diameter. This sight stunned me. I knew to a certainty that the only way for that space to open was for people to swarm back over the top of those behind them, manhandling each other out of the way.

Bill Wyman: "We would be halfway through a song, and suddenly there was some commotion over there, and the Angels were beating the shit out of some guy. The crowd would open, and you would see six Angels just whacking them with pool cues, and you thought, *What's going on?* It just went on like that. Every two or three minutes something was going on in the crowd, or the side of the stage, or somewhere. It just got worse and worse. You couldn't walk off the stage. You couldn't just stop when all these people had come to see you."

Stanley writes, Keith set out on "Sympathy for the Devil" as Mick sang, "I was 'round when Jesus Christ / Had his moment of doubt and pain." There was a low explosive *thump!* in the crowd to the right of the stage, and oily blue-white smoke swirled up. People were pushing, falling, a great hole opening as they moved instantly away from the center of the trouble. I had no idea people in a crowd could move so fast. Mick stopped singing but the music chugged on, four bars, eight, and then Mick shouted, "Hey! Heeey! Keith-Keith-Keith!" By now only Keith was playing, but he was playing as loud and as hard as ever, the way the band is supposed to do. "Will you cool it and I'll try and stop it," Mick said, so Keith stopped.

For me, looking down on it all from my perch on the truck, things were happening that didn't compute. There was no precedent in my experiences for the scenes I kept seeing. It seemed to drag on and on while I kept expecting Mick to stop it, somehow. I naively believed he had the power and was disappointed he seemed so timid. Keith, much bolder, tried to put a stop to it—and then was told someone in the audience had a gun and was shooting at the stage.

That someone was Meredith Hunter, a young black man from Oakland. He had come to the concert in his black Mustang accompanied by Patty Bredehoft, a seventeen-year-old white girl. Early on he told Patty that he was going back to the car, that he wanted his gun in case there was any trouble.

At his car Hunter retrieved a long-barreled .22-caliber pistol from the trunk, stuck it into his waistband, and covered it with his coat. He returned to the concert and, as it got darker and the Rolling Stones were about to perform, he made his way toward the stage. There were still swarms of people on the stage, including many Hells Angels. Wave after wave of violence swept through the crowd, causing people to be jammed against each other.

The music stopped again, and Sam Cutler announced that the Rolling Stones would not perform

> "There was a low explosive *thump!* in the crowd to the right of the stage, and oily blue-white smoke swirled up. People were pushing, falling, a great hole opening as they moved instantly away from the center of the trouble."
>
> STANLEY BOOTH

Meredith Hunter (in a green coat, to the left of the Hells Angel) at the lip of the stage.

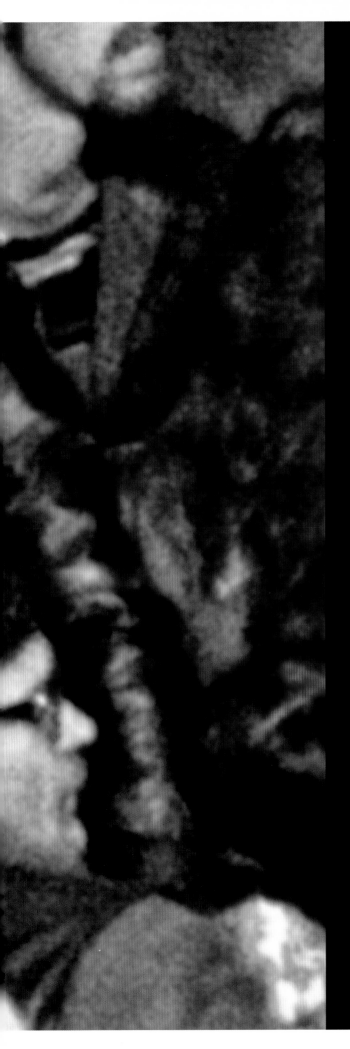

After being at the concert for a short time Meredith Hunter tells his girlfriend Patty Bredehoft that he wants his gun in case there is any trouble. He goes back to his car and retrieves a long-barreled .22 caliber from the trunk which he places in his waistband.

The next thing Bredehoft saw was an altercation with six or seven Hells Angels. Hunter tried to get away to the right of the stage, where he pulled a gun.

"That is when he's told by another Angel, 'Look, man, a guy's got a gun out there and he's shooting at the stage.'"
STANLEY BOOTH

"**Mick Taylor and I saw the whole thing** and then my heart skipped a beat and I felt nauseous because I knew someone had been seriously hurt."

BILL WYMAN

until the stage was cleared. Patty watched as Hunter got involved in trying to get people off the speaker boxes in front of the stage.

The next thing Patty saw was Hunter arguing and scuffling with six or seven Hells Angels. Hunter tried to get away to the right of the stage but was hemmed in and then blocked by the crowd. At bay, he turned and pulled his gun.

Alan Pasarro, a Hells Angel standing near the stage, saw the gun. He pulled a five-inch knife and stabbed it deep into Meredith Hunter's back. Then he brought up his arm and slammed the knife into Hunter again. And again.

Bill Wyman: "Mick Taylor and I were the ones nearest to it. We saw the crowd open and the guy chase the other guy right in front of us. We both saw the commotion when the guy got stabbed. We saw the whole thing, and then my heart skipped a beat, and I felt nauseous because I knew someone had been seriously hurt."

Stanley writes, An Angel in front of the stage was trying to tell Keith something, but Keith wouldn't listen. Keith said, "I don't like you to tell me . . . Look, we're splitting, if those cats . . . if those people don't stop beating up everybody in sight—I want 'em out of the way!" But that is when he is told by another Angel, "Look, man, a guy's got a gun out there, and he's shooting at the stage."

Ronnie says, "I was running for the ambulance when a cop stopped me. He said, 'You don't need to run anymore—he's dead.' "

Toward stage right.
The feeling of
devastation at
Altamont was total.

PART IV: AFTERMATH

Gimme Shelter

"It was the most dangerous, most frightening show we ever did, and this band has never been scared of anything."

BILL WYMAN

When Meredith Hunter was stabbed I must have still been on the top of the truck. I remember Keith calling out, "If those cats don't stop, we're splitting." I thought, *Finally, someone saying something.* I wasn't aware there had been a stabbing. It was just another one of the unholy holes opening up, people scrambling away from onrushing Hells Angels. It wasn't until I saw the Maysles' film, *Gimme Shelter,* that I actually saw it. I could barely watch the film, so vividly did it recall the time at Altamont. Looking at the stabbing, I felt as if I'd been kicked in the stomach, and I was depressed for days.

Mick finally spoke up, his voice traveling out over the whole mass of people, but really aimed at the rows right in front of him, the ones you could see, where the beatings were, before the lights from the stage surrendered to the bigger darkness: "It seems to be stuck down to me. Will you listen to me for a minute? Please *listen to me* for just one second, al'right? San Francisco, is like the whole thing—everyone—*come on* now. You know, this could be the most beautiful evening we've had this winter . . . don't let's fuck it up, man, come on— let's get it together—If we are all *one*, let's show we're all *one!*"

It seemed a plaintive cry given the level of violence. But it didn't occur to me then—I was so naive— that Mick's life was in danger, too. In the film, I could see a man, crazed on some unknown mixture of drugs, whose eyes were quite literally bulging out of his head, staring straight at Mick, his hands clenching and unclenching themselves, pulling at his hair, his face contorted. He's clearly stoned, violent, and precipitately murderous, and he was standing not eight feet from Mick.

After his plea Mick continued, "Now there's one thing we need, Sam. We need an ambulance." But, as Ronnie said, it was too late.

Not long after Mick's call I dropped off the top of the truck and began my scramble into the darkness and up the hill, wanting nothing more than to get out of there.

Bill Wyman: "It was the most dangerous, most frightening show we ever did, and this band has never been scared of anything. Well. Maybe twice, but Altamont was the worst because you did think something serious could happen. They would beat the band up or something because we didn't have any security. There was no security anywhere. It was like a nightmare. It was like it wasn't reality. You were in a dream, a bad dream."

Jo Bergman: "We were taken up the hill to the helicopter, and I had this feeling that it was all like you were the last person on the last chopper out of 'Nam."

Astrid: "We knew that the helicopter we were on was the last one out of there. By the time we got to the helicopter the girlfriend of the guy who got stabbed was outside. The cops were with her.

Opposite: Bill Wyman, looking terrified, arriving at the helicopter, the only way out.

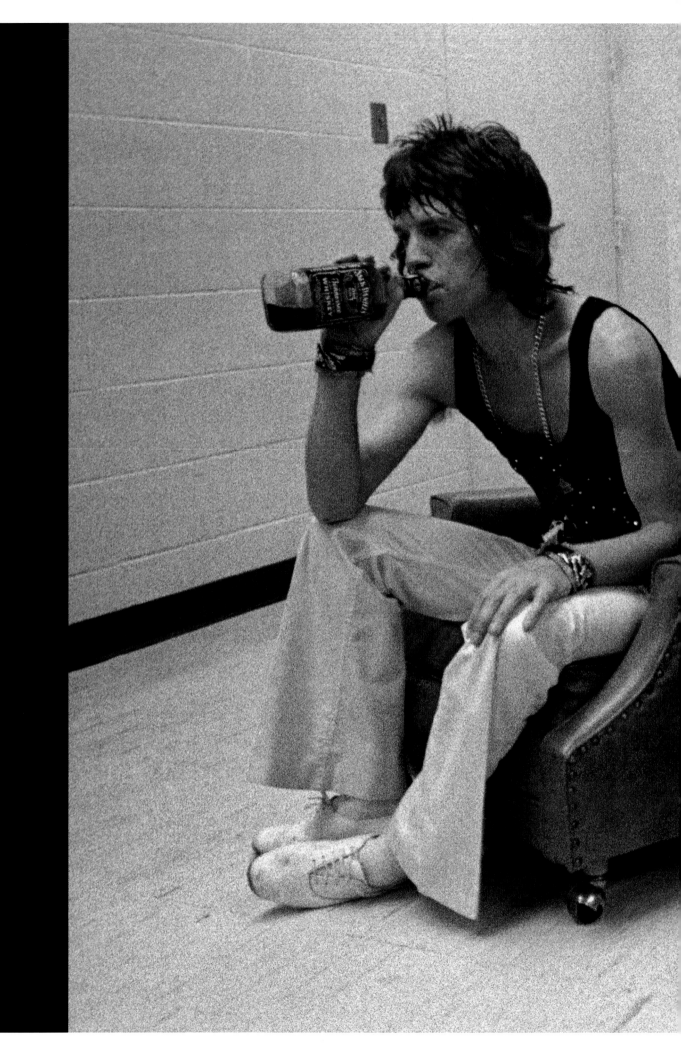

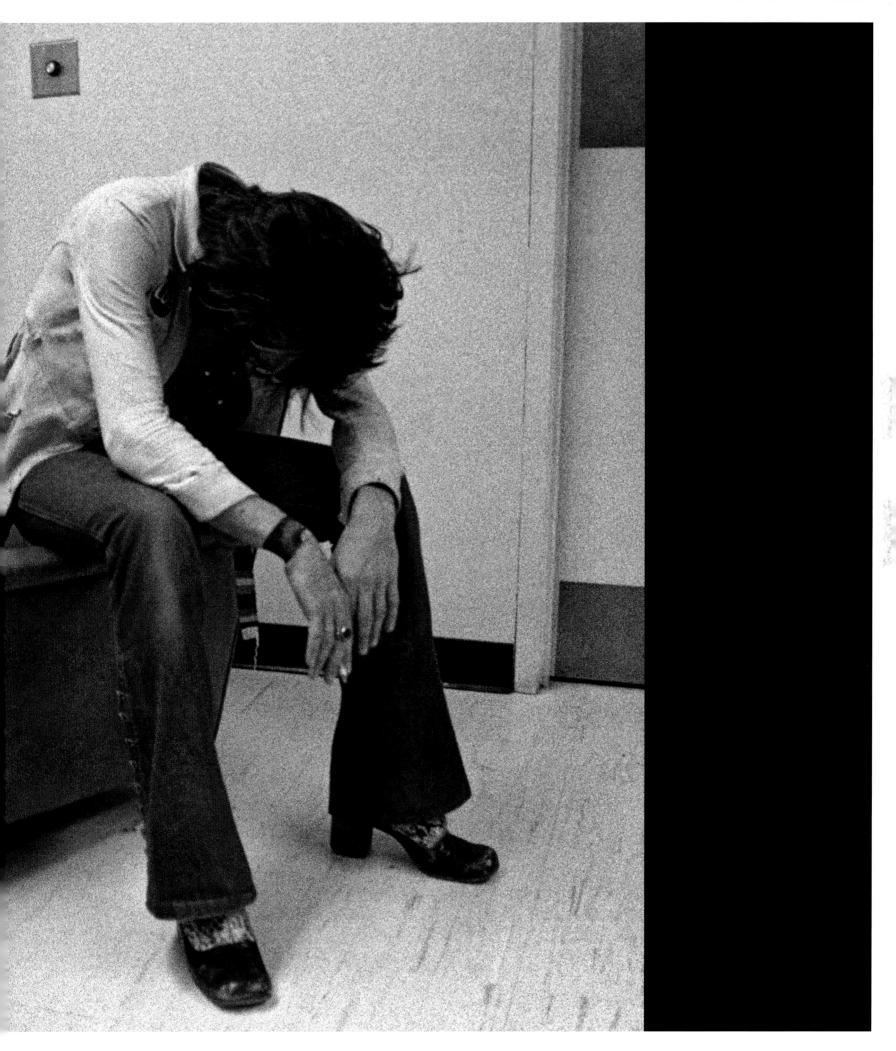

"It was a miracle we weren't all killed," says Georgia Bergman. "There were so many ways to die."

Escaping. People that will leave in this one helicopter: The pilot, Mick Jagger, Keith Richards, Bill Wyman, Astrid Lundstrom, Mick Taylor, Charlie Watts, Gram Parsons, Michelle Phillips, Sam Cutler, Ethan Russell, Georgia Bergman, Ronnie Schneider, David Horowitz, Stanley Booth, unknown woman, unknown man.

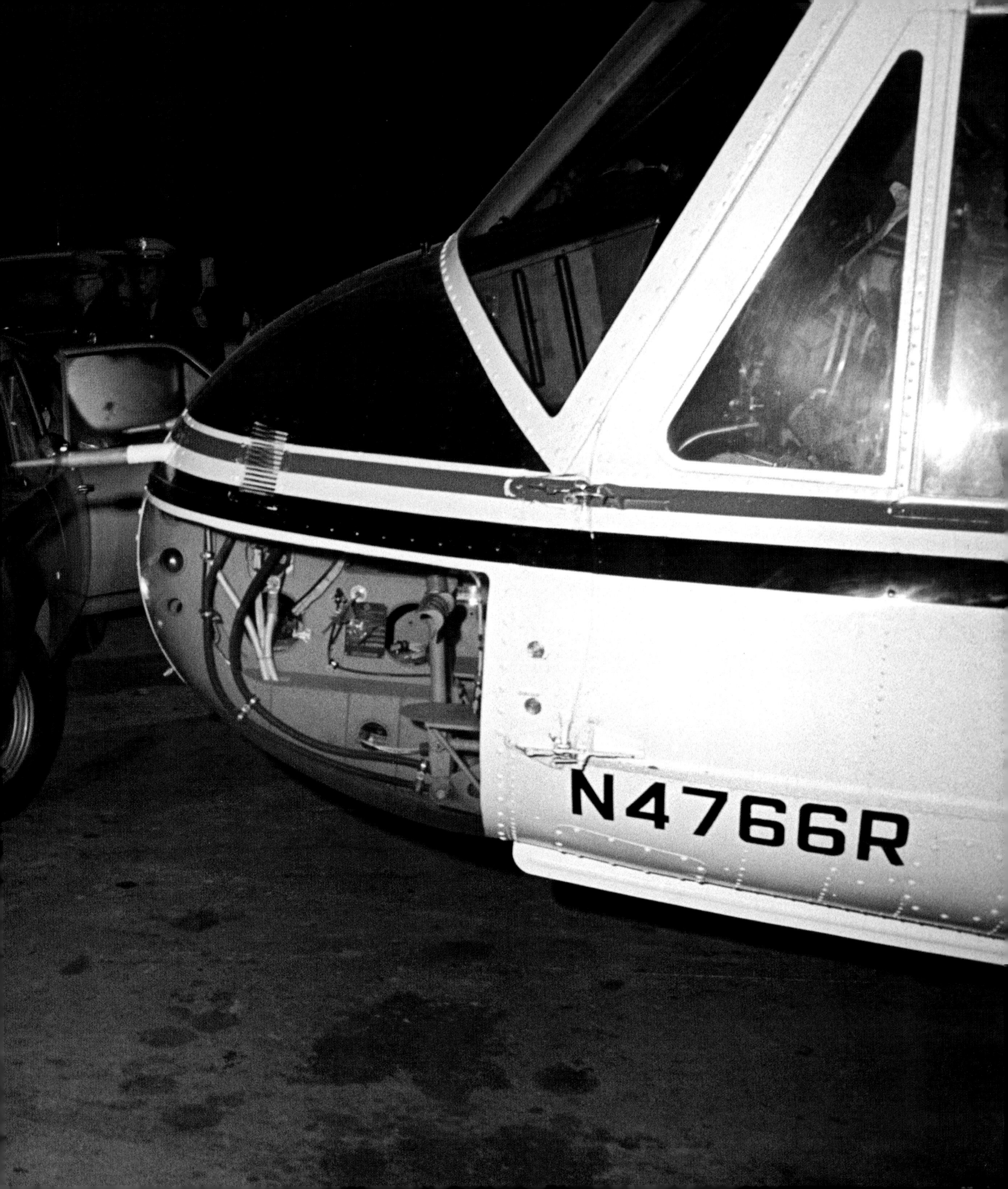
N4766R

She was hysterical; she was saying things like, 'Is he dead?' She was totally freaking out. Then the music stopped and everybody suddenly rushed toward the helicopter. It was unbelievable. I couldn't believe how many people were coming in."

Stanley: "I ended up with Gram in the darkness, trying to climb up this hillside. There were people everywhere. We were yelling out to each other just to try to stay together and climbed over or through that fence—somehow we got across it—and got to a place where they had station wagons. We got in a station wagon and some of Jon Jaymes's guys drove us up to where the helicopters were. Everybody was climbing into that helicopter—eighteen people, something like that. I'm thinking, *Oh Jesus, what are we going to do if they leave without us?* and Sam says, 'Gram! Stanley!' I got on. You would have been crazy if you hadn't been scared."

And so the helicopter began its spastic liftoff into the night. We are jammed in, people sitting in other people's laps, lying on the floor. Total on board? Mick Jagger, Keith Richards, Bill Wyman, Astrid Lundstrom, Mick Taylor, Charlie Watts, Gram Parsons, Michelle Phillips, Sam Cutler, Jo Bergman, Ronnie Schneider, David Horowitz, Stanley Booth, unknown woman, unknown man, the pilot, and me.

While most of us are on the helicopter, others remain. Chip Monck had long known that he would have to stay behind and clean up the mess. And the violence was not over. "After the helicopter left, I started to clean up. I rolled up the rug, put it on one side of the stage, and went to find guys to help me put it in the truck. But first I had to go after my cables and get my lighting down. All of a sudden I look up and see the rug driving away in the back of a pickup, stuck on the roof, hanging across the tailgate, almost touching the ground. I ran and grabbed one end of the rug and it went bump on the ground. Unfortunately it pulled a Hells Angels chopper out of the back with it. Three Hells Angels got out of the cab. We had four to five minutes of civil conversation. I kept saying, 'I hope you'll excuse me. Let me explain to you what my job is. You guys did your job. I have to complete my job. I have no malice, nothing between us except that you have a piece of Mick Jagger's property, and I am responsible for it.' Then they whacked me across the mouth. I lost two teeth."

Astrid, who escaped on the helicopter, says, "Afterwards I don't remember anyone talking about it. I remember them being more like in shock. There was none of that usual bravado, none of the put-down, of making light of something in a sarcastic way. When we left people were still in shock. I don't think the full impact of it hit them totally until they saw it on film. It was a very, very dark thing."

Jo Bergman: "I remember the *Rolling Stone* article about Altamont, which blamed the Stones. To them it was all the Stones' fault. To me, it seemed unfair. The Stones themselves had no idea. It was the sixties, dammit. Weird things happened and people did things and asked questions later.

"But then how could they have known? How would those people know that Mick and Keith weren't on a planning committee—if there even was a planning committee—or that they weren't completely involved in every last detail of every single thing that was going on?"

Bill Wyman: "I know it must seem strange that no one has talked about it, but basically I didn't want to relate back to it. I just wanted to forget it. The chaos of the earlier tours was fun—a laugh, really.

But no one really talked about Altamont because there was nothing to laugh about. There were no good memories at all."

In an interview for a San Francisco radio station Mick Jagger remarked, "I thought the scene in San Francisco was supposed to be so groovy. I don't know what happened; it was terrible. If Jesus had been there he would have been crucified."

PEOPLE BACKED OFF, RETREATED FROM THE BIG IDEAS, headed for the hills, sometimes literally, and a lot of people took more and more drugs.

Stanley Booth: "At Altamont the wind went out of our sails and people split to the hills, I went to the hills, and people started taking more drugs than ever before. Tequila and cocaine and all that fog. The tour ended so traumatically. It just seemed a very hard place to go on from. I remember Mick saying when the Maysles brothers were over in London working on the film, 'I don't want to show something that's just a bummer.'

"I don't know what it would have been if Altamont hadn't happened, but it seemed to me that the thrust of my generation's idealistic intention had just gone off the cliff. It wasn't just Altamont. It was the whole thing. That fall, Keith was talking about the festivals, and what good things they were, and the idea that we could end the war, that people who felt the way we did were growing in numbers, that we were having an influence in the political world, which was unprecedented as far as we knew, that it looked as though we were going to really be able to make a difference. Then we have a free concert and California turns into Vietnam. Not only can we not make a difference, we can't even have a fucking free show without it turning into a disaster."

Michael Lydon: "It was unpleasant, to say the least. And it was disappointing. How can this be? We're powerless. We've been naive and haven't understood. That stayed with me: The naive idealism of twenty-four- and twenty-five-year-olds is not going to change the world. It's good for you personally, but it's not going to change the world.

"I woke up the next day and just as Altamont had been on everyone's lips before it happened, afterwards everyone was talking about it. Now people said it was the anti-Woodstock, the end of the sixties. And in truth for me and for many other people it was the end of the sixties, the end of freedom, and love, and 'vibes are gonna get us all the way.' For me it meant going more private, living quietly, living small. These other aspirations were too huge. They weren't going to work. So going small was the direction I wanted to go."

The morning after Altamont I woke up in the hotel and, as I remember, everyone was gone except Sam Cutler, who was still upstairs in his room, still wearing the white sweater stained with Meredith Hunter's blood.

I moved on. I was busy. I was a full-time photographer now, shooting the Who and others, flying back and forth from America. In 1972 I would return to shoot the Rolling Stones again. But something in me (it is probably not too much to say) died at Altamont as well. Without the conversation Michael

Lydon refers to, it fell silent. There was plenty of activity. The rock 'n' roll that I loved, driven by that new entity—the singer/songwriter—remained rich for a while, but it was fading. The Eagles, alluding to the end, sang "Call someplace paradise, kiss it good-bye," and thereafter their music turned to the preoc-

cupations of the seventies: cocaine and a fast hedonism. "A room full of noise and dangerous boys still makes you thirsty and hot." Even John Lennon would exclaim: "Don't give me no more brother, brother."

It's interesting to me that the divide between those who think Altamont was the end of the sixties and those who don't falls almost entirely along national lines, between the Americans and the English sensibilities, echoing the political disconnect that dogged us through the whole tour. Americans of my generation almost exclusively see Altamont as the event that ended the sixties, while the British seem to think the entire notion hyperbolic. Mick Taylor, in a beautiful example, responded when asked if he thought Altamont was the end of the sixties, "Well it was the end of the sixties, wasn't it? It was December 1969." And Mick Jagger would sing in a song that I have always thought was explicitly meant to distance him from all that the sixties represented: "It's only rock 'n' roll, but I like it."

History uses markers. D-day didn't end the Second World War, but it was the beginning of the end, and in that

sense, it was a marker. So it is with Altamont. Even those that disagree with the label don't dispute the fact that the feeling of devastation at Altamont was total, both while you were there and afterwards, as if everything had collapsed. Call it what you will.

EPILOGUE

Not Fade Away

In early February 2007 I returned to the Altamont Speedway. I hadn't been back since the helicopter lifted us out on that December evening in 1969.

After I'd moved back to San Francisco in 1992, I'd sometimes drive to Los Angeles via the quickest route that led over the Altamont Pass to connect with Interstate 5. In the pass I'd gaze out the windows at the hills, knowing somewhere among them was the Speedway, but not knowing exactly where. Every so often on these trips I'd get off the freeway and wander the feeder roads hoping to stumble across it, but I never did. There was always a ghostly feeling to these excursions. I didn't know what I was looking for, and wasn't sure I wanted to find it.

But when it came time to write this book, I knew I had to go back to the site. So I called the Speedway and made an appointment to meet Jim Becker, the Altamont concessions manager. That morning, in the way of this era, I googled "Altamont Speedway," got driving directions, and printed out a map.

Today, after you turn away from the waters of San Francisco Bay, US 580 takes you east through the sprawl of Pleasanton and Livermore. From the freeway you see only the bedroom developments and shopping malls with the large chains: Bed Bath & Beyond, Staples, and Target. Past Livermore, the towns fade out and the hills take over.

I drove over the summit of the Altamont Pass and down the other side, exited at Grant Line Road, and turned left under the freeway. Once off the freeway it reverted to the old landscape of tan and barren California hillsides and falling-down fences. The only big change was the hundreds of windmills meant to capture the winds as they crossed back and forth from the Central Valley to the Bay. Except for these wind farms, the landscape remained the same.

The gate to the (now renamed) Altamont Motorsports Park was open, and I drove through. There was a new set of shaded stands that the company's Web site boasted could handle up to 7,500 spectators. I pulled through the open gate and drove down a slight incline into a large parking lot, empty except for a pickup down near the track.

The pickup belonged to Jim Becker, a pleasant man in his fifties, who handled concessions and lived at the track as a kind of watchman when the NASCAR events weren't running. I introduced myself. Becker told me he was from Southern California, and he'd been a racing aficionado since he was a kid. He'd moved up north to work at Altamont. He introduced me to his wife, who did floral decorations.

As we walked around, Jim brought me up to speed on the recent history of Altamont, told me they'd added a small inner track inside the main one and a lot of new paint.

I looked around. The fields and hills surrounding Altamont were empty, brown, and scraggly, just like in 1969. We walked out into them. I'd brought along some shots I'd taken showing the hills packed with the crowds in 1969. It took a little time, but soon we were able to orient ourselves and make out where we were and where the stage would have been.

I kept hearing the sound of diesel trucks downshifting in the distance. I didn't remember that from the day of the concert. It took me awhile to realize why the sound seemed so alien. There had been no sound. The freeway had been a parking lot in 1969, filled with abandoned cars.

I walked through the dry grass and dirt, taking pictures. To be there seemed resonant and yet dull and distant. Jim told me stories of the concert that people had told him. The stories were a mix of the apocryphal and the untrue. In the stands where he took me later, he showed me two "posters" from the concert, both fakes manufactured after the event—one with a picture of Mick from 1972. Over the years, friends of mine have reported seeing these Altamont posters framed and displayed in stores and restaurants as far away as Maine. There are, of course, no original posters of the "Altamont Festival." There wasn't enough time to print them.

Becker and I walked slowly down the hillside where the hundreds of thousands had been camped out. The dry grass crackled under my feet. California hadn't had much rain that winter, and the ground was parched. It was cold, too.

We finally arrived at the bottom of the bowl, where the stage must have been. Once I knew that I could start to figure out where Meredith Hunter must have been when he'd been killed.

I looked back up at the hillside stretching away. Behind me occasional carcasses of cars jutted from the landscape, rusting, just as in '69. Except for the traffic bending around the track to the north and flowing south, a rushing buzz with the occasional backing-off riprap of a semi shifting down, there wasn't any soundtrack.

Making conversation, Becker said, "You know, I've heard there's some talk of doing a commemorative concert in 2009. Fortieth anniversary . . . like they did for Woodstock."

"Really?" I said. "I don't know about that. There probably aren't a lot of good memories that would motivate people to come."

"That's probably true," he said. "Maybe they'll just get someone to donate some kind of plaque we could put up on the grandstand. You know, a memorial kind of thing. I've heard people talk about that, too, but so far nothing's come of it."

STANDING WHERE THE STAGE HAD BEEN, I could only imagine the sweep of the hundreds of thousands filling the amphitheater. I didn't have a visual memory, because by the time I'd gotten to the stage in 1969 it was night and most of the immense crowd had been hidden beyond the stage-lights in the dark. Meredith Hunter would have been out there as well, but closer than most. Lots of people that day had walked in with hope and belief in a shared vision of a better world, and while there witnessed hours of violence. Hunter had come with a gun and he'd never walked out at all.

Altamont today.

Later, when he blows up these images, he discovers that they conceal a body that lies just at the edge of what the enlargement of details in his pictures can reveal.

Becker and I walked up the brown hill that I'd scrambled up in the darkness trying to get back to the helicopter. It was as if my body had a memory of the slope because it was easy to remember struggling up it and easy to remember the helicopter sitting there.

I'd expected to spend more time at Altamont, staying at least until sundown. But having walked the site, there didn't seem much reason to stick around. I stood on the top row of seats of the newly painted grandstand looking back over the hills. I took a picture. Then I drove slowly home, not listening to anything on the radio.

When I got to Livermore—where in 1969 the helicopter had bounced to the ground and dispersed everyone back to the hotel in San Francisco—I was absorbed by lanes of cars, shopping malls, and massive cineplexes. It snapped me back into the present. It didn't seem like much had been added, besides people, in the last forty years.

In 1967, as a young man wondering what I might do with myself, I had wandered the fields of Golden Gate Park taking pictures. I was emulating scenes from the movie *Blow-Up*, by Michelangelo Antonioni. It starred David Hemmings as Thomas, a successful fashion photographer in the "swinging London" of those years. One day, on a lark, Thomas takes a series of pictures of a pair of lovers in a park. Later, when he blows up these images, he discovers that they conceal a body that lies just at the edge of what the enlargement of details in his pictures can reveal.

Obsessed by his discovery, Thomas goes back to the park and finds the body. He leaves to get a witness, but when Thomas returns to the scene, the body has disappeared. All the photographer has to prove it existed is a collection of blown-up photographs whose grainy dots, viewed from a distance, could be one thing or another.

Blow-Up was a seminal movie for me at that moment in my life. Filmed in London, it was full of style, beautiful women, and mystery. Opening and closing the movie was a band of colorful, white-faced actors jammed into an old truck, careening through the streets and raising a ruckus. In an eerie real-world parallel San Francisco's 1967 Human Be-In, "the gathering of the tribes" in Golden Gate Park, was like an entire football field of these colorful players.

In Antonioni's movie, people are smoking a lot of hash and staring into space, soporific and glassy-eyed. Simultaneously, in San Francisco, drugs were swiftly moving beyond marijuana and a little (sacramental) LSD to become more powerful and pervasive, including methamphetamine, heroin, and that old standby, alcohol. The call for "Higher!" was everywhere.

And, Antonioni seemed to say, we might have a slight problem with reality. What happened in the park, despite the ability of the camera to capture what's real, remains a mystery. In the movie's closing scene, Thomas is watching the white-faced actors playing tennis, their heads panning as their eyes track the ball back and forth, back and forth. They watch the ball accidentally fly over the tall fence surrounding the court and land on the grass. They signal to Thomas to return it. He pauses for a moment, looking quizzical, but then he bends over, picks up the ball, and throws it back. The players thank him

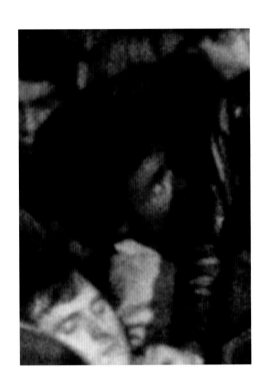

and resume their game. Only: there is no ball. Not in the tennis game, and not on the grass for Thomas to throw back. Never was.

In time, I became the photographer. I lived in London and loved it. I worked with most of the greatest musical artists of our time. When, after Altamont the spirit drifted out of music (for whatever reason and whatever you say), so did I, though missing both.

As I edited the photographs for this book I found myself (now using digital technology, drum scans, and computers) poring over the film and slides of Altamont. Like Thomas I was blowing them up, peering into the shadows and along the edges of the frame, looking for Meredith Hunter, who I had not even known was there.

I found Hunter in only two photographs. In one he is made up of fuzzy balls of grain (if it weren't for his lime green suit you would not know for certain that it was him). And then in another image, found only weeks before the book would go to the printer, Hunter stands at the very lip of the stage, staring up at someone on a speaker. Today the camera would record the exact moment of the shot, but not then. Still, in time measured in minutes, not hours, from when I took the picture, Meredith Hunter would no longer be with us.

After Altamont many, as Stanley Booth said, "split for the hills." Alan Passaro, the Angel who stabbed Meredith Hunter, was brought to trial and acquitted. Meredith Hunter had a gun, after all, and was pointing it at the stage. The moment, caught forever in the Maysles film, is blurry and indistinct, but that's what it looks like. It was the ultimate act of violence (you could even argue, as some do, that Alan Pasarro saved Mick Jagger's life), but it was only one of many violent acts from an entire afternoon of beatings, screams, and hopelessness in this, the latest of our vaunted free festivals.

No one ever really took responsibility for what happened at Altamont. Not the Angels, not the people in the crowd, not the Rolling Stones. Each person involved seemed to conclude, each with their own reason, that somehow what happened had nothing—or very much less than the other guy—to do with them.

The memory of *Blow-Up* made me wonder what it meant when an event like we had at Altamont—something massive, cataclysmic, and generation-shattering—left no visible sign. It was like the murdered body in *Blow-Up*. Thomas goes back to find it and it's gone. Just the wind in the trees.

The Rolling Stones kept going farther and for longer than anyone, including themselves, had any right to expect. The same thing that kept us going through the drudgery of touring—"That sense of *Oh my God, we get to see them perform*," as Jo Bergman said— was the thing that endeared them to the ages.

As Astrid Lundstrom recalls, "I saw thousands of concerts. And I can say in all that time that a concert never bored me. Being on tour might have, but the concert? Never. They were always amazing."

Acknowledgments

I'll start by thanking the Rolling Stones, particularly the two earliest line-ups of the band: the original with Brian Jones and the second with Mick Taylor. As much as I'm still a fan of the Rolling Stones, the first two were my bands, whose music I listened to over and over. I also want to acknowledge their remarkable longevity. In the annals of "Who Would've Ever Guessed?" this simple fact, and not so simple achievement, must rank near the top.

I wish to thank, too, all those who helped with this book, particularly those who shared their stories and allowed me to create something with a deeper perspective than if I had to rely on my experiences alone. They include Georgia "Jo" Bergman, Stanley Booth, Sam Cutler, Tony Funches, Glyn Johns, Astrid Lundstrom, Michael Lydon, Chip Monck, Ronnie Schneider, Mick Taylor, and Bill Wyman. Of these Stanley Booth deserves special mention since his work *The True Adventures of the Rolling Stones* remains, in my opinion (to use the words of Peter Guralnick), "the one authentic masterpiece of rock 'n' roll writing."

In this edition, Gerard Van der Leun also needs to be singled out. Not only does he share writing credit, he is also the mystery "friend" who came to England in 1968 and introduced me to Jonathan Cott, who asked me if I wanted to photograph Mick Jagger. This single event changed my life. Another old friend, Andy Caulfield, oversaw the scanning, preperation, and retouching of all the photographs used in the book. I couldn't have done it without him.

I wish to thank Roger Gorman for his design. From Springboard Press I wish to thank Karen Murgolo, editorial director; Tom Hardej, assistant editor; Matthew Ballast, executive director of publicity; Pamela Schechter, production manager; Tareth Mitch, production editor; and Mark Steven Long and Roland Ottewell, copy editors. I wish to thank Alan Nevins for his agenting.

In addition, I want to thank the team at Rhino for their initial and ongoing support: Scott Pascucci, David Dorn, Marc Salata, John Beug, and Kathy Rivkin.

And finally, I wish to thank my family, Shannon, Gabriel, and Lucas, for their love.